CARROLL

BOYD K. PACKER

BOOKCRAFT

Salt Lake City, Utah

Only standard works, official statements, and other
publications written under assignment from the
First Presidency and the Council of the Twelve Apostles
are considered authorized publications by
The Church of Jesus Christ of Latter-day Saints.
Other publications, including this one,
are the responsibility of the writer.

The Author

Library of Congress Catalog Card Number 98-74086
ISBN 1-57008-582-X

First Printing, 1998

Printed in the United States of America

Put on the whole armour of God, that ye may be able to stand against the wiles of the devil. . . . Above all, taking the shield of faith, wherewith ye shall be able to quench all the fiery darts of the wicked.

—Ephesians 6:11, 16

Contents

PART ONE   *Family*

1   The Father and the Family   3
2   Where Is Your Power?   9
3   The Shield of Faith   15
4   Little Children   22
5   The Moving of the Water   30

PART TWO   *Priesthood*

6   The Great Witness from These Conferences   39
7   The Twelve Apostles   45
8   "Come, All Ye Sons of God"   53

PART THREE   *Learning*

9   The Gospel—The Foundation for Our Career   63
10 "To Be Learned Is Good If . . ."   71
11 Language of the Spirit   79
12 Personal Revelation: The Gift, the Test,
       and the Promise   84
13 Gifts of the Spirit   92

PART FOUR   *Agency*

14   The Choice   *113*
15   Our Moral Environment   *120*
16   Agency and Control   *128*
17   The Word of Wisdom: The Principle and
           the Promises   *134*

PART FIVE   *Holiness*

18   The Holy Temple   *143*
19   Washed Clean   *152*
20   The Brilliant Morning of Forgiveness   *160*
21   A Temple to Exalt   *168*

         Index   *187*

PART ONE

Family

1

The Father and the Family

A FAMILY BEGINS WHEN A YOUNG MAN and woman are drawn to one another by an irresistible force of nature. They offer to one another that which distinguishes him as male and her as female, and they want, above all else, to find the one with whom they can completely express their love. They want to have children—to be a family.

These compelling forces of nature should not be resisted, only approached cautiously, protecting those life-generating powers until promises have been made to one another, covenants with the Lord, and a legal ceremony performed, witnessed, and recorded.

Then, and only then, as husband and wife, man and woman, may they join together in that expression of love through which life is created.

The ultimate purpose of every teaching, every activity in the Church, is that parents and their children are happy at home, sealed in an eternal marriage, and linked to their generations.

The ultimate purpose of the adversary, who has "great wrath, because he knoweth that he hath but a short time" (Revelation 12:12), is to disrupt, to disturb, and to destroy the home and the family. Like a ship without a rudder, without a compass, we drift from the family values which have anchored us in the past. Now we are caught in a current so strong that unless we correct our course, civilization as we know it will surely be wrecked to pieces.

Moral values are being neglected and prayer expelled from public schools on the pretext that moral teaching belongs to religion.

Address given at general conference April 1994.

3

At the same time, atheism, the secular religion, is admitted to class, and our youngsters are proselyted to a conduct without morality.

World leaders and court judges agree that the family must endure if we are to survive. At the same time, they use the words *freedom* and *choice* as tools to pry apart the safeguards of the past and loosen up the laws on marriage, abortion, and gender. In so doing, they promote the very things which threaten the family.

None of this is new. Jacob, the Book of Mormon prophet, told the people of Nephi: "I . . . am weighed down with much more desire and anxiety for the welfare of your souls than I have hitherto been. . . . It grieveth me that I must use so much boldness of speech concerning you, before your wives and your children, many of whose feelings are exceedingly tender and chaste and delicate before God." (Jacob 2:3, 7; see vv. 1–13.)

This crisis of the family is no surprise to the Church. We have certainly known what was coming.

I know of no better testimony that we are led by prophets than our preparation for this present emergency.

The scriptures speak of prophets as "watch[men] upon the tower" who see "the enemy while he [is] yet afar off" (D&C 101:54; see vv. 45, 53–54; 2 Kings 9:17) and who have "beheld also things which were not visible to the natural eye . . . [for] a seer hath the Lord raised up unto his people" (Moses 6:36; see also Mosiah 8:15–17).

Thirty-three years ago the Brethren warned us of the disintegration of the family and told us to prepare. It was announced by the First Presidency and the Quorum of the Twelve Apostles that the Church would be restructured.

The weekly family home evening was introduced by the First Presidency, who said that "the home [is] the basis of a righteous life and . . . no other instrumentality can take its place nor fulfil its essential functions" (in Conference Report, October 1961, p. 79; *Improvement Era*, January 1962, p. 36).

Parents are provided with excellent materials for teaching their children, with a promise that the faithful will be blessed (see

"Message from the First Presidency," *Family Home Evening Resource Book* [Salt Lake City: The Church of Jesus Christ of Latter-day Saints, 1983], p. iv).

While the doctrines and revealed organization remain unchanged, all agencies of the Church have been reshaped in their relationship to one another and to the home.

So sweeping were those changes that the entire curriculum of the Church was overhauled—based on scriptures, with excellent manuals for each course.

And years were spent preparing new editions of the Bible, the Book of Mormon, the Doctrine and Covenants, and the Pearl of Great Price. Except for correcting printing errors and adding three revelations to the Doctrine and Covenants, the scriptural text remains unchanged.

Cross-references and other helps were added to make the scriptures more accessible. In the Topical Guide, for instance, under the heading of "Jesus Christ" there are eighteen pages—small print, single-spaced—the most comprehensive compilation of scriptural references on the Lord that has ever been compiled in the history of the world.

The new editions of the scriptures are complete in English and Spanish, and work is now under way in dozens of languages.

We can only imagine where we would be if we were just now reacting to this terrible redefinition of the family. But that is not the case. We are not casting frantically about trying to decide what to do. We know what to do and what to teach.

The family is very much alive and well in the Church. Hundreds of thousands of happy families face life with an unwavering faith in the future.

The course we follow is not of our own making. The plan of salvation, the great plan of happiness, was revealed to us, and the prophets and Apostles continue to receive revelation as the Church and its members stand in need of more.

We, like Jacob, must teach "according to the strict commands of God," "notwithstanding the greatness of the task." Like Jacob, we also run the risk of enlarging "the wounds of those who are

already wounded, instead of consoling and healing their wounds."
(Jacob 2:9–10.)

When we speak plainly of divorce, abuse, gender identity, contraception, abortion, parental neglect, we are thought by some to be way out of touch or to be uncaring. Some ask if we know how many we hurt when we speak plainly. Do we know of marriages in trouble, of the many who remain single, of single-parent families, of couples unable to have children, of parents with wayward children, or of those confused about gender? Do we know? Do we care?

Those who ask have no idea how much we care; you know little of the sleepless nights, of the endless hours of work, of prayer, of study, of travel—all for the happiness and redemption of mankind.

Because we *do* know and because we *do* care, we must teach the rules of happiness without dilution, apology, or avoidance. That is our calling.

I once learned a valuable lesson from a mission Relief Society president. In a conference, she announced some tightening up of procedures. A sister stood up and defiantly said: "Those rules can't apply to us! You don't understand us! We are an exception."

That wonderful Relief Society president replied: "Dear sister, we'd like not to take care of the exception first. We will establish the rule first, and then we'll see to the exception." Many times I have borrowed from her wisdom, grateful for what she taught me.

Now, following the example of Jacob, I speak to the men of the Church. Most of you are worthy fathers and husbands who do what you should do. But there are women whose hearts have been broken (see Jacob 2:35) and children who are neglected, even abused.

If we are to help them, we must begin with the men. Stake and regional conferences have been devoted to teaching the doctrines and principles of responsible and worthy manhood.

Some of you had no worthy example to follow and now visit the abuse or neglect of your own parents upon your wife and children.

Brethren, do you understand that we emphasize the teaching of the scriptures because they are the constant? From them we learn the purposes of life, the gifts of the Spirit. From them we learn about personal revelation, how to discern good from evil, truth from error. The scriptures provide the pattern and the basis for correct doctrine.

From doctrine, we learn principles of conduct, how to respond to problems of everyday living, even to failures, for they, too, are provided for in the doctrines.

If you understand the great plan of happiness and follow it, what goes on in the world will not determine your happiness. You will be tried, for that is part of the plan, but "thine afflictions shall be but a small moment; and then, if thou endure it well, God shall exalt thee on high" (D&C 121:7–8).

Your responsibility as a father and a husband transcends any other interest in life. It is unthinkable that a Latter-day Saint man would cheat on his wife or abandon the children he has fathered, or neglect or abuse them.

The Lord has "commanded you to bring up your children in light and truth" (D&C 93:40; see vv. 36–40).

You are responsible, unless disabled, to provide temporal support for your wife and children (see D&C 83:2). You are to devote yourself, even sacrifice yourself, to the bringing up of your children in light and truth (see D&C 93:40).

That requires perfect moral fidelity to your wife, with no reason ever for her to doubt your faithfulness.

Never should there be a domineering or unworthy behavior in the tender, intimate relationship between husband and wife (see D&C 121:41–43).

Your wife is your partner in the leadership of the family and should have full knowledge of and full participation in all decisions relating to your home.

Lead your family to the Church, to the covenants and ordinances. We are trying to reduce the length and number of meetings and activities outside of the home.

I cannot express the depth of my devotion to my wife and

children, their companions, and their children. I have learned more by far from them than they from me. That learning comes in ordinary experiences, the joy and the pain of everyday life.

The family is safe within the Church. We are not in doubt as to the course we must follow. It was given in the beginning, and guidance from on high is renewed as need may be.

As we continue on our course, these things will follow as night the day:

The distance between the Church and a world set on a course which we cannot follow will steadily increase.

Some will fall away into apostasy, break their covenants, and replace the plan of redemption with their own rules.

Across the world, those who now come by the tens of thousands will inevitably come as a flood to where the family is safe. Here they will worship the Father in the name of Christ, by the gift of the Holy Ghost, and know that the gospel is the great plan of happiness, of redemption.

2

Where Is Your Power?

SOME TIME AGO I STOOD AT THE BEDSIDE of an aged little Danish woman. She was near the close of her life. There was a serenity and anticipation, even a beauty about her as she talked of what soon would be.

There stood with us her middle-aged son, a pathetic figure. He had lost his wife and family through self-indulgence and for the past number of years had been living at home with his aged mother. Tearfully he pleaded, "Mama, you can't go. Mama, you've got to live. Mama, you can't die."

Now, as the last person who seemed to care much for him at all was about to go home, his pleadings became almost frantic as he demanded, "Mama, you can't go." And then he said with emphasis, "Mama, I won't let you go."

I have not forgotten her response. The little mother looked up at her son, and in her broken Danish accent she said, "But vher iss yoa powah?" Her question, "Where is your power?" should provoke introspection in all of us.

Her son had brought no honor to the family name. As a father he had failed. How sharper than a serpent's tooth is failure such as this!

The Church of Jesus Christ of Latter-day Saints is a family-centered church. I bear fervent, solemn witness that The Church of Jesus Christ of Latter-day Saints was divinely instituted; that there stands at the head of this Church today a prophet of God, and that the program of the Church is ordered by revelation from

_____
Address given at general conference October 1963.

on high. In the Church there is reverence for family relationships. Family relationships are sacred. The family is eternal.

I devote this chapter to fathers in recognition of their place at the head of the home. A home evening program has been inaugurated in the Church. It reaffirms to every father his responsibility. It brings to every father new opportunity.

The responsibilities of fatherhood cannot be delegated to social agencies, nor even to the Church, for a father may unwittingly erase all of the good effects of those outside the home who seek to build for him a worthy son.

Parents frequently call upon the General Authorities of the Church and anxiously argue that we are the last hope to rescue a wayward son or daughter. They seek a blessing we cannot always bestow, for often we find it is the parent and not the child that needs reproof. How wise was the prophet when he said: "The fathers have eaten sour grapes, and the children's teeth are set on edge" (Ezekiel 18:2).

One cannot, I repeat, escape the obligation of fatherhood. The father who neglects his son may suffer the condemnation that the Lord placed upon the prophet Eli when He said: "For I have told him that I will judge his house forever for the iniquity which he knoweth; because his sons made themselves vile, and he restrained them not" (1 Samuel 3:13).

I would remind you that the father is first of all a husband, and essential to the rearing of fine stalwart sons is proper regard for the wife and the mother of the family. O how important it is for a son to have a proper relationship with his father and with his mother, and for him to know that his father and his mother live together in love. There are some hideous things that can happen to a boy—ugly, abnormal, perverted things. A proper parental pattern is the greatest insurance against tragedy such as this.

The prophet Jacob, in accusing wayward fathers of his day, said: "Behold, ye have done greater iniquities than the Lamanites, our brethren. Ye have broken the hearts of your tender wives, and lost the confidence of your children, because of your bad examples before them; and the sobbings of their hearts ascend up to God against you." (Jacob 2:35.)

If the father does not honor the priesthood he holds, rest assured that the son will do more than duplicate the inactivity. He will likely magnify the mischief he sees in you, Father. Fortunately, the same may be true of your virtue and activity also.

Give careful, prayerful, conscious thought and consideration to your family. Do not bury your life in merely providing a living. Many men play the role of fatherhood just by ear. They only react to what is, rather than to strive with conscious, prayerful effort for what ought to be.

A necessary and important discovery with reference to a boy is that he is an individual. Boys must be taught to work, but boys are not miniature men, and the Lord has urged: "And, ye fathers, provoke not your children to wrath: but bring them up in the nurture and admonition of the Lord" (Ephesians 6:4).

A boy is not born to know that his father loves him. He must be told and shown and shown and told a thousand times or more. A father must be wise and patient, but most of all he must be consistent, and his expectations must be reasonable. For as the poet said:

> What unjust judges fathers are, when in regard to us
>   they hold
> That even in our boyish days we ought in conduct
>   to be old.
> Nor taste at all the very things that youth and only youth
>   requires;
> They rule us by their present wants, not by their past
>   long-lost desires.
> (Terence, *The Self-Tormentor,* trans. F. W. Ricord, act 1,
> scene 3.)

Years ago a Church leader described a lecture he had given his children. He had forcefully affirmed to them how he had been self-sufficient as a youth, how dependable he had been, how hard he had worked. His tiny daughter brought him back to earth by saying, "Daddy, when you were a little baby, did you fix your own bottle?"

Where is your power to rear children to bring honor to your name? Each father would do well to recognize that he is himself a son. This is true in an eternal way. It is my testimony that the word *father* in the scriptures means father; that we have a child-parent relationship with God; that we were created in His image; that we are His children, and each one of us, particularly those who hold the priesthood, will one day have to answer to Him.

The late President George Albert Smith once lay critically ill. Those close to him despaired of his life. He later recorded:

> One day, under these conditions, I lost consciousness of my surroundings and thought I had passed to the Other Side. I found myself standing with my back to a large and beautiful lake, facing a great forest of trees. There was no one in sight, and there was no boat upon the lake or any other visible means to indicate how I might have arrived there. I realized, or seemed to realize, that I had finished my work in mortality and had gone home. I began to look around, to see if I could not find some-one. . . .
>
> . . . Soon I found a trail through the woods which seemed to have been used very little, and which was almost obscured by grass. I followed this trail, and after I had walked for some time and had traveled a considerable distance through the forest, I saw a man coming towards me. I became aware that he was a very large man, and I hurried my steps to reach him, because I recognized him as my grandfather. . . .

(His grandfather was George A. Smith, First Counselor to President Brigham Young.) President Smith continues:

> I remember how happy I was to see him coming. I had been given his name and had always been proud of it.

When Grandfather came within a few feet of me, he stopped. His stopping was an invitation for me to stop. Then—and this I would like the . . . people never to forget—he looked at me very earnestly and said:

"I would like to know what you have done with my name."

Everything I had ever done passed before me as though it were a flying picture on a screen—everything I had done. Quickly this vivid retrospect came down to the very time I was standing there. My whole life had passed before me. I smiled and looked at my grandfather and said:

"I have never done anything with your name of which you need be ashamed."

He stepped forward and took me in his arms, and as he did so, I became conscious again of my earthly surroundings. My pillow was as wet as though water had been poured on it—wet with tears of gratitude that I could answer unashamed. (*Sharing the Gospel with Others* [Salt Lake City: Deseret Book Co., 1948], pp. 111–12.)

This vision or dream of President Smith reminds each of us of the responsibility we bear with reference to the name that has been given us. We have taken upon ourselves the name of Christ and have entered into a covenant to remember Him always and to keep the commandments which He has given us, and in consequence of keeping the commandments there comes a promise that we shall have His Spirit to be with us.

Our measure will not depend on academic degrees or political preference or property or influence so much as simply how we lived at home. To be a worthy father is to be a faithful son. The formula for either is the same.

Where is your power? It is in the power of example. Where is your power to raise sons to do honor to your name? It is in the power of the priesthood.

Here are a few lines from Jane Terry, written to teachers, applicable to fathers who are the teachers of their sons:

You are called to be true under-shepherds,
To keep watch o'er the lambs of the fold,
And to point out the way to green pastures
Of more value than silver or gold.

Unto you are entrusted the children,
Priceless treasures from heaven above;
You're to teach them the truth of the gospel,
Let them bask in the warmth of your love.

Do you ask for the help of our Father
In teaching his children so dear?
Do you put forth a true, honest effort?
Is your message impressive and clear?

Are you living a worthy example?
Is your character what it should be?
When the children have gathered around you,
Can you say, "Come, follow me"?

Earnest effort is always rewarded,
Righteous lives are inspiring to all;
You can render your thanks to our Savior
By making the most of your call.

3

The Shield of Faith

WHEN PRESIDENT EZRA TAFT BENSON passed away, without a pause the brief and memorable administration of President Howard W. Hunter began. God bless the memory of that great prophet. Again, without the slightest pause, the order of things confirmed in the revelations was implemented with all of our participation, and the Church moves forward on course.

This practice of raising hands to sustain one who has been called to lead or to teach in the Church is a matter of sacred importance. The voting to sustain takes place in meetings, and the sustaining of the First Presidency, now broadcast to the Church across the world, conforms to a revelation from the Lord:

> I say unto you, that it shall not be given to any one to go forth to preach my gospel, or to build up my church, except he be ordained by . . . one who has authority, and *it is known to the church* that he has authority and has been regularly ordained by the heads of the church (D&C 42:11; emphasis added).

Speaking for the Quorum of the Twelve Apostles, who "agreeable to the institution of heaven" are "to officiate in the name of the Lord, under the direction of the Presidency of the Church" (D&C 107:33), we affirm to you that in sustaining President Gordon B. Hinckley and his counselors, our First Presidency, the Twelve is one. For in raising our hands to sustain the President of the Church, we continue the line of unbroken authority from the beginning of the Restoration.

Address given at general conference April 1995.

15

The Twelve Bridge the Line of Authority

Some suppose that the keys of presidency pass from one man to another much like a baton in a relay. Some believe that the Prophet Joseph Smith secretly or privately conferred the keys of presidency upon a successor. But that is not the order of things. President Ezra Taft Benson did not ordain Howard W. Hunter as President of the Church, nor did President Howard W. Hunter ordain Gordon B. Hinckley as President of the Church.

The Twelve bridge the line of authority from one administration to another and keep the line unbroken.

Shortly before the Martyrdom, in a meeting attended by nine members of the Twelve, the Prophet Joseph Smith prophetically said:

> Brethren, the Lord bids me hasten the work in which we are engaged. Some important scene is near to take place. It may be that my enemies will kill me. And in case they should, and the keys and power which rest on me not be imparted to you, they will be lost from the earth. But if I can only succeed in placing them upon your heads, then let me fall a victim to murderous hands if God will suffer it, and I can go with all pleasure and satisfaction, knowing that my work is done, and the foundation laid on which the kingdom of God is to be reared in this dispensation of the fulness of times. Upon the shoulders of the Twelve must the responsibility of leading this church henceforth rest until you shall appoint others to succeed you. (Draft Declaration of the Twelve Apostles, reporting March 1844 meeting of the Twelve, Brigham Young papers, LDS Church Archives.)

Individually and collectively the Twelve hold the keys and have confirmed the authority to exercise all of the keys upon the senior Apostle, the one man who is to preside over the Church.

The Lord has provided a system in which there is no aspiring, no maneuvering for position or power, not even a hint of soliciting for votes or cultivating influence. The system does not allow it, nor would the Lord permit it. It does not work the way man usually works, and so it should be. The Lord reminded the prophet Isaiah, "My ways [are] higher than your ways, and my thoughts than your thoughts" (Isaiah 55:9).

SUSTAINING THE PROPHET

The raising of the hands has been a custom since ancient times, symbolized when Moses was confronted by the Amalekite robbers, the destroyers of the wilderness:

> Moses said unto Joshua, Choose us out men, and go out, fight with Amalek: to morrow I will stand on the top of the hill with the rod of God in mine hand.
>
> So Joshua did as Moses had said to him, and fought with Amalek: and Moses, Aaron, and Hur went up to the top of the hill.
>
> And it came to pass, when Moses held up his hand, that Israel prevailed: and when he let down his hand, Amalek prevailed.
>
> But Moses' hands were heavy; and they took a stone, and put it under him, and he sat thereon; and Aaron and Hur stayed up his hands, the one on the one side, and the other on the other side; and his hands were steady until the going down of the sun.
>
> And Joshua discomfited Amalek and his people with the edge of the sword. (Exodus 17:9–13.)

The wicked who now oppose the work of the Lord, while different from, are no less terrible than, the plundering Amalekites. The sustaining of the prophet is still an essential ongoing part of the safety of this people. Should age and infirmity cause his hands to grow heavy, they are held up by his counselors at his side. Both are prophets, seers, and revelators, as is each member of the Quorum of the Twelve.

"We Are Living Apostles of the Lord"

In 1976, following a conference in Copenhagen, Denmark, President Spencer W. Kimball invited us to a small church to see the statues of Christ and the Twelve Apostles by Bertel Thorvaldsen. The Christus stands in an alcove beyond the altar. Standing in order along the sides of the chapel are the statues of the Twelve, with Paul replacing Judas Iscariot.

President Kimball told the elderly caretaker that at the very time Thorvaldsen was creating those beautiful statues in Denmark, a restoration of the gospel of Jesus Christ was taking place in America, with Apostles and prophets receiving authority from those who held it anciently.

Gathering those present closer to him, he said to the caretaker, "We are living Apostles of the Lord Jesus Christ," and pointing to Elder Pinegar he said, "Here is a Seventy like those spoken of in the New Testament."

We were standing near the statue of Peter, whom the sculptor depicted holding keys in his hand, symbolic of the keys of the kingdom. President Kimball said, "We hold the real keys, as Peter did, and we use them every day."

Then came an experience I will never forget. President Kimball, this gentle prophet, turned to President Johan H. Benthin, of the Copenhagen Stake, and in a commanding voice said, "I want you to tell every prelate in Denmark that they do NOT hold the keys! I HOLD THE KEYS!"

There came to me that witness known to Latter-day Saints but difficult to describe to one who has not experienced it—a light, a power coursing through one's very soul—and I knew that, in very fact, here stood the living prophet who held the keys.

Apostles Bring Unity of the Faith

The Lord revealed why "he gave some, apostles; and some, prophets." It is "for the perfecting of the saints, for the work of the ministry, for the edifying of the body of Christ: till we all come in the unity of the faith, and of the knowledge of the Son of God." (Ephesians 4:11–13.)

The ministry of the Apostles—the Presidency and the Twelve—therefore is to bring us to a unity of the faith.

As it has been since the beginning, the adversary would divide us, break us up, and, if he can, destroy us. But the Lord said: "Lift up your hearts and rejoice, and gird up your loins, and take upon you my whole armor, that ye may be able to withstand the evil day, . . . taking the *shield of faith* wherewith ye shall be able to quench all the fiery darts of the wicked" (D&C 27:15, 17; emphasis added).

The ministry of the prophets and Apostles leads them ever and always to the home and the family. That shield of faith is not produced in a factory but at home in a cottage industry.

The ultimate purpose of all we teach is to unite parents and children in faith in the Lord Jesus Christ, that they are happy at home, sealed in an eternal marriage, linked to their generations, and assured of exaltation in the presence of our Heavenly Father.

THE SHIELD OF FAITH IS MADE AT HOME

Lest parents and children be "tossed to and fro" and misled by "cunning craftiness" of men who "lie in wait to deceive" (Ephesians 4:14), our Father's plan requires that, like the generation of life itself, the shield of faith is to be made and fitted in the family. No two can be exactly alike. Each must be handcrafted to individual specifications.

The plan designed by the Father contemplates that man and woman, husband and wife, working together, fit each child individually with a shield of faith made to buckle on so firmly that it can neither be pulled off nor penetrated by those fiery darts.

It takes the steady strength of a father to hammer out the metal of it and the tender hands of a mother to polish and fit it on. Sometimes one parent is left to do it alone. It is difficult, but it can be done.

In the Church we can teach about the materials from which a shield of faith is made: reverence, courage, chastity, repentance, forgiveness, compassion. In church we can learn how to assemble and fit them together. But the actual making of and fitting on of the shield of faith belongs in the family circle. Otherwise it may loosen and come off in a crisis.

The prophets and Apostles know full well that the perilous times Paul prophesied for the last days are now upon us: "Men [are] lovers of their own selves, covetous, boasters, proud, blasphemers, disobedient to parents, unthankful, unholy, without natural affection" (2 Timothy 3:2–3).

Knowing it would be so, the Lord warned that

> Inasmuch as parents have children in Zion, or in any of her stakes . . . , that teach them not to understand the doctrine of repentance, faith in Christ the Son of the living God, and of baptism and the gift of the Holy Ghost . . . , the sin be upon the heads of the parents.
>
> For this shall be a law unto the inhabitants of Zion. . . .
>
> And they shall also teach their children to pray, and to walk uprightly before the Lord. (D&C 68:25–26, 28.)

As stated earlier, this shield of faith is not manufactured on an assembly line, only handmade in a cottage industry. Therefore our leaders press members to understand that what is most worth doing must be done at home. Some still do not see that too many out-of-home activities, however well intended, leave too little time to make and fit on the shield of faith at home.

GOD'S PLAN FOR HAPPY FAMILIES

Although our thoughts may tend to be centered on the noble titles High Priest, President, Apostle, Prophet, Seer, Revelator, the heavens are not offended if we speak of father, mother, child, brother, sister, family—even dad, mom, grandma, grandpa, baby.

If you are reverent and prayerful and obedient, the day will come when there will be revealed to you why the God of heaven has commanded us to address Him as *Father,* and the Lord of the Universe as *Son.* Then you will have discovered the pearl of great price spoken of in the scriptures and will willingly go and sell all that you have that you might obtain that pearl.

The great plan of happiness (see Alma 42:8, 16) revealed to prophets is the plan for a happy family. It is the love story of husband and wife, parents and children, that renews itself through the ages.

And so with an unbroken line of priesthood authority, an unbroken line of priesthood power, we move confidently forward in unity and faith, led by Christ the Redeemer, whose church this is, and His earthly prophet, through whom He will speak.

4

Little Children

Some years ago Dr. Faun Hunsaker, then president of the Southern States Mission, was invited to stay at the home of a member. He arrived after the children were in bed.

He occupied the parents' bedroom, and during the night heard the door open and the sound of little feet. A little boy frightened by a bad dream had come to his parents' bed for comfort.

Sensing that something was different, the little boy felt Brother Hunsaker's face. So he spoke quietly to the child. The startled youngster said, "You're not my daddy!"

"No, I'm not your daddy."

"Did my daddy say you could sleep here?"

"Yes, your daddy said I could sleep here."

With that the little youngster crawled into bed with Brother Hunsaker and was soon asleep.

My purpose here is to moralize about innocence and our obligation to little children.

There is much in the scriptures about little children.

The Psalmist wrote, "Children are an heritage of the Lord" (Psalm 127:3).

The Savior gave the ever-familiar plea, "Suffer little children, and forbid them not to come unto me; for of such is the kingdom of heaven" (Matthew 19:14).

When His disciples asked, "Who is the greatest in the kingdom of heaven? . . . Jesus called a little child unto him, and set him in the midst of them, and said, . . . Whosoever . . . shall humble

---

Address given at general conference October 1986.

himself as this little child, the same is greatest in the kingdom of heaven. And whoso shall receive one such little child in my name receiveth me." (Matthew 18:1–5.)

Then came this warning: "But whoso shall offend one of these little ones which believeth in me, it were better for him that a millstone were hanged about his neck, and that he were drowned in the depth of the sea" (v. 6).

To me, the most impressive lesson is in the Book of Mormon.

[Jesus] commanded that their little children should be brought.

So they brought their little children and set them down upon the ground round about him, and Jesus stood in the midst; . . .

He commanded the multitude that they should kneel down upon the ground.

And it came to pass that when they had knelt upon the ground, Jesus groaned within himself, and said: Father, I am troubled because of the wickedness of the people of the house of Israel. . . .

He himself also knelt upon the earth; and behold he prayed unto the Father, and the things which he prayed cannot be written, . . .

And no tongue can speak, neither can there be written by any man, neither can the hearts of men conceive so great and marvelous things as [they] both saw and heard Jesus speak; . . .

And they arose from the earth, and he said unto them: Blessed are ye because of your faith. And now behold, my joy is full.

And when he had said these words, he wept, and the multitude bare record of it, and he took their little children, one by one, and blessed them, and prayed unto the Father for them.

And when he had done this he wept again;

And he . . . said unto them: Behold your little ones. . . .

And they saw the heavens open, and they saw angels descending out of heaven as it were in the midst of fire; and they came down and encircled those little ones about, and they were encircled about with fire; and the angels did minister unto them. (3 Nephi 17:11–15, 17, 20–24.)

There is more, much more, in the scriptures about little children.

There is a sorry side to this subject as well. I wish not to dwell on that beyond listing four transgressions which plague mankind, all of which inflict suffering upon little children.

First, that consummate physical union of man and woman belonging to the marriage covenant is now falsely proclaimed an acceptable indulgence for any two adults.

Second, the misuse of that procreative power in degraded acts of perversion is widely promoted as the right of consenting adults. This selfish behavior carries neither the responsibility nor the rewards of parenthood.

Third, the deliberate destruction of the innocent and helpless by abortion is now widely fostered—even publicly funded.

Fourth, the bodies and minds and morals of increasing numbers of little children are brutalized and abused by those who should protect them.

In it all, mankind has sown a bitter wind and reaps heartbreak, guilt, abandonment, divorce, addiction, disease, and death; and little children suffer.

If these sins remain unchecked, civilization will be led unfailingly to destruction.

Our behavior is not totally controlled by natural impulses. Behavior begins with belief as well.

Beliefs are born of philosophies, of doctrines. Doctrines can be spiritual or secular, wholesome or destructive, true or false.

Two doctrines misrepresent the status of little children. Each is widely accepted. Both are false!

The first holds that little children are conceived in sin and enter mortality in a state of natural corruption. That doctrine is false!

Each time a child is born, the world is renewed in innocence.

The revelations teach us that:

The glory of God is intelligence, or, in other words, light and truth.

Light and truth forsake that evil one.

Every spirit of man was *innocent* in the beginning; and God having redeemed man from the fall, men became again, in their infant state, *innocent* before God.

And that wicked one cometh and taketh away light and truth, through disobedience, from the children of men, and because of the tradition of their fathers.

But I have commanded you to bring up your children in light and truth. (D&C 93:36–40; emphasis added.)

Mormon taught this doctrine to his son Moroni and hence to us. Only a few sentences from his letter are cited here.

"If I have learned the truth," Mormon wrote, "there have been disputations among you concerning the baptism of your little children" (Moroni 8:5).

He called their disputation a "gross error" and wrote:

Immediately after I had learned these things of you I inquired of the Lord concerning the matter. And the word of the Lord came to me by the power of the Holy Ghost, saying:

Listen to the words of Christ, your Redeemer, your Lord and your God. Behold, I came into the world not to call the righteous but sinners to repentance; the whole need no physician, but they that are sick; wherefore, little children are whole, for they are not capable of committing sin; wherefore the curse of Adam is taken from them in me, that it hath no power over them; . . .

And after this manner did the Holy Ghost manifest the word of God unto me; wherefore, my beloved son, I know that it is solemn mockery before God, that ye should baptize little children. (Moroni 8:7–9.)

Mormon told Moroni to teach repentance and baptism to "those who are accountable and capable of committing sin" (Moroni 8:10).

Eight is established by revelation as the age of accountability
(see D&C 18:42; 68:27).

In sternness unsurpassed in scripture, Mormon warned:

> He that supposeth that little children need baptism is in the
> gall of bitterness and in the bonds of iniquity; for he hath neither
> faith, hope, nor charity; wherefore, should he be cut off while in
> the thought, he must go down to hell.
>
> For awful is the wickedness to suppose that God saveth one
> child because of baptism, and the other must perish because he
> hath no baptism.
>
> Wo be unto them that shall pervert the ways of the Lord after
> this manner, for they shall perish except they repent. Behold, I
> speak with boldness, having authority from God. (Moroni
> 8:14 16.)

Read his entire epistle. It is true doctrine. It will inspire a reverence for little children. Thereafter, who could even think to neglect, much less to abuse, one of them?

True doctrine, understood, changes attitudes and behavior.

The study of the doctrines of the gospel will improve behavior
quicker than a study of behavior will improve behavior. Preoccupation with unworthy behavior can lead to unworthy behavior.
That is why we stress so forcefully the study of the doctrines of
the gospel.

The laws of God on marriage, birth, and nurturing of little
children may seem rigid, but they are very practical.

His law decrees that the only legitimate union of man and
woman is between husband and wife. For, should that expression
of love result in conception, marriage provides shelter for the
child who enters mortality innocent and helpless. Marriage en-
sures security and happiness for parents as well.

Whatever the laws of man may come to tolerate, the misuse of
the power of procreation, the destroying of innocent life through
abortion, and the abuse of little children are transgressions of
enormous proportions. For cradled therein rests the destiny of innocent, helpless children.

Another doctrine, equally false and widely accepted, also misrepresents the status of little children. Let me illustrate.

Years ago, two of our sons, then little fellows, were wrestling on the rug. They reached that line which separates laughter from tears, so I worked my foot carefully between them and lifted the older one back to a sitting position on the rug. As I did so, I said, "Hey there, you little monkeys. You'd better settle down."

To my surprise, he folded his little arms, his eyes swimming with deep hurt, and protested, "I not a monkey, Daddy; I a *person!*"

The years have not erased the overwhelming feeling of love I felt for my little boys. Many times over the years his words have slipped back into my mind, "I not a monkey, Daddy; I a *person!*" I was taught a profound lesson by my little son.

He is not just a person, nor just my little boy. He is a child of God.

The cycle of life has moved swiftly on. Now both of those sons have little children of their own who teach their fathers lessons. They now watch their children grow as we watched them. They are coming to know, as fathers, something they could not be taught as sons.

All too soon their children will be grown with little "persons" of their own, repeating the endless cycle of life.

Perhaps now they understand what it means to begin our prayers, as the Lord instructed, "Our Father who art in heaven." He is our father; we are His children.

Secular doctrine holds that man is not a child of God, but basically an animal, his behavior inescapably controlled by natural impulse, exempt from moral judgments and unaccountable for moral conduct.

While many claim that this philosophy could not, in the end, lead mankind to relaxed moral behavior, *something* causes it! Is it accidental that the more widely such secular doctrines are believed, the more prevalent immoral behavior becomes?

They defend their philosophy with collected data and say: "It is now proven to be true. Look at all the evidence on our side."

We in turn point to the sorry way in which mankind degrades

procreation and the attendant suffering of both children and adults and say, "Look at all the evidence on our side."

Secular doctrines have the advantage of convincing, tangible evidence. We seem to do better in gathering data on things that can be counted and measured.

Doctrines which originate in the light, on the other hand, are more often supported by intangible impressions upon the spirit. We are left for the most part to rely on faith.

But, in time, the consequences of following either will become visible enough.

To you adults who repeat the pattern of neglect and abuse you endured as little children, believing that you are entrapped in a cycle of behavior from which there is no escape, I say:

It is contrary to the order of heaven for any soul to be locked into compulsive, immoral behavior with no way out!

It *is* consistent with the workings of the adversary to deceive you into believing that you *are*.

I gratefully acknowledge that transgressions, even those which affect little children, yield to sincere repentance. I testify with all my soul that the doctrine of repentance is true and has a miraculous, liberating effect upon behavior.

To you innocent ones who have not transgressed, but were abused as little children and still carry an undeserved burden of guilt, I say:

Learn true doctrine—repentance *and* forgiveness; lay that burden of guilt down!

For we are all children of the same Heavenly Father. May not each of His children, of any age, claim the redeeming sacrifice of Jesus Christ, and in so doing, through complete repentance, be cleansed and renewed to childlike innocence?

I conclude with the account of that trusting little child I spoke of at the beginning.

"You're not my daddy."

"No, I'm not your daddy."

"Did my daddy say you could sleep here?"

"Yes, your daddy said I could sleep here."

With that, the little boy was soon safely asleep in his arms.

God grant that all little children will be safe with every one of us because their Father and their God and our Father and our God said we could be here.

5

The Moving of the Water

"Now there is at Jerusalem by the sheep market a pool, which is called in the Hebrew tongue Bethesda, having five porches.

"In these lay a great multitude of impotent folk, of blind, halt, withered, waiting for the moving of the water.

"For an angel went down at a certain season into the pool, and troubled the water: whosoever then first after the troubling of the water stepped in was made whole of whatsoever disease he had." (John 5:2–4.)

There has always been in all of humanity a sprinkling of those who are described in the scriptures as the blind, the halt, the lame, the deaf, the withered, the dumb, the impotent folk. We refer to them as having learning or communication disorders, as the hearing or visually impaired, as those with motor or orthopedic limitations. We speak of intellectual or emotional impairment, of retardation, and mental illness. Some suffer from a combination of these, and all of them cannot function without some help.

I reach out to the families of those who, at birth or as the result of accident or disease, must live with an impaired body or mind. I desire to bring comfort to those to whom the words *handicapped* or *disability* have very personal meaning.

It is my intent to teach doctrine which, if understood, will reinforce your courage and endurance, even foster a measure of contentment with circumstances which you did not invite, do not deserve, but from which you cannot turn away.

Address given at general conference April 1991.

No Room for Guilt

I must first, and with emphasis, clarify this point: It is natural for parents with handicapped children to ask themselves, "What did we do wrong?" The idea that *all* suffering is somehow the direct result of sin has been taught since ancient times. It is false doctrine. That notion was even accepted by some of the early disciples until the Lord corrected them.

> As Jesus passed by, he saw a man which was blind from his birth.
> And his disciples asked him, saying, Master, who did sin, this man, or his parents, that he was born blind?
> Jesus answered, Neither hath this man sinned, nor his parents: but that the works of God should be made manifest in him. (John 9:1–3.)

There is little room for feelings of guilt in connection with handicaps. Some handicaps may result from carelessness or abuse, and some through addiction of parents. But most of them do not. Afflictions come to the innocent.

The very purpose for which the world was created, and man introduced to live upon it, requires that the laws of nature operate in cold disregard for human feelings. We must work out our salvation without expecting the laws of nature to be exempted for us. Natural law is, on rare occasions, suspended in a miracle; but mostly our handicapped, like the lame man at the pool of Bethesda, wait endlessly for the moving of the water.

Never Ridicule

It is not unusual for foolish children and some very thoughtless adults to make light of the handicapped. The mimicking or teasing or ridiculing of those with handicaps is cruel. Such an assault can inflict deeper pain than can physical punishment—more painful because it is undeserved. It is my conviction that such brutality will not, in the eternal scheme of things, go unanswered, and there will come a day of recompense.

My mother taught us when we were very young that we must never ridicule the unfortunate. Her mother died when she was six. My mother worked in the fields from a very early age. One day some teenagers were picking fruit. One of the girls laughingly mimicked one who suffered from cerebral palsy, saying, "Look who I am," and she named the handicapped person. They all laughed as she threw herself into a stumbling walk.

Suddenly she fell as if struck down. They gathered around her in great fright. Presently she recovered, but there was no more fun at the expense of the handicapped. Mother never forgot what she saw, nor to teach a lesson from it.

Parents, take time in the next home evening to caution your family never to amuse themselves at the expense of the handicapped or of any whose face or form or personality does not fit the supposed ideal or whose skin is too light or too dark to suit their fancy. Teach family members that they, in their own way, should become like angels who "move the water," healing a spirit by erasing loneliness, embarrassment, or rejection.

In Mendoza, Argentina, we attended a seminary graduation. In the class was a young man who had great difficulty climbing ordinary steps. As the class marched in, two strong young classmates gracefully lifted him up the steps. We watched during and after the proceedings, and it became apparent that the whole class was afflicted with a marvelous kind of blindness. They could not see that he was different. They saw a classmate, a friend. In *them* the works of God *were being* manifest. While there was no physical transformation in the boy or in his classmates, they were serving like angels, soothing a spirit locked in a deformed body awaiting that time when it would be made everlastingly perfect.

SHE'S UNDER THERE SOMEWHERE

At a stake conference I noticed on the front row a family including a girl of ten who had palsy and was deaf. Her father held her so that she would not slide off the bench. Their tenderness touched me deeply. When the meeting ended, I motioned for them to come up to me, for they were holding back. The father turned so that I could see Heidi's face, which was buried into his shoulder, and he said with a smile, "She's under there someplace."

Indeed she is under there someplace. All of them are under there somewhere.

President Joseph Fielding Smith explained that "all spirits while in the pre existence were perfect in form, having all their faculties and mental powers unimpaired. . . . Deformities in body and mind are . . . physical." (*Answers to Gospel Questions,* comp. Joseph Fielding Smith, Jr., 5 vols. [Salt Lake City: Deseret Book Co., 1979], 3:19.) *Physical* means "temporal"; *temporal* means "temporary." Spirits which are beautiful and innocent may be temporally restrained by physical impediments.

If healing does not come in mortal life, it will come thereafter. Just as the gorgeous monarch butterfly emerges from a chrysalis, so will spirits emerge.

> Their sleeping dust [will] be restored unto its perfect frame, bone to his bone, and the sinews and the flesh upon them, the spirit and the body to be united never again to be divided, that they might receive a fulness of joy (D&C 138:17).

And

> The soul shall be restored to the body, and the body to the soul; yea, and every limb and joint shall be restored to its body; yea, even a hair of the head shall not be lost; but all things shall be restored to their *proper* and *perfect* frame (Alma 40:23; emphasis added).

O how great the plan of our God! . . . the spirit and the body is restored to itself again, and all men become incorruptible, and immortal, and they are living souls, having a perfect knowledge like unto us in the flesh, save it be that our knowledge shall be perfect. (2 Nephi 9:13.)

The Apostle Paul said: "If in this life only we have hope in Christ, we are of all men most miserable" (1 Corinthians 15:19).

If our view is limited to mortal life, some things become unbearable because they seem so unfair and so permanent. There are doctrines which, if understood, will bring a perspective toward and a composure regarding problems which otherwise have no satisfactory explanation.

Truth: We are spirit children of a Father God. We lived with Him in our premortal existence, of which it must be said that there was not, neither could there have been, a beginning. The revelations speak of things "from before the foundation of the world" and "before the world was." (See D&C 124:33–41.)

Truth: Mortal life is temporary and, measured against eternity, infinitesimally small. If a microscopic droplet of water should represent the length of mortal life, by comparison all the oceans on earth put together would not even begin to represent everlasting life.

Truth: After mortal death we will rise in the resurrection to an existence to which there will not, neither could there be, an end. The words *everlasting, never-ending, eternal, forever and forever* in the revelations describe both the gospel and life.

That day of healing will come. Bodies which are deformed and minds that are warped will be made perfect. In the meantime, we must look after those who wait by the pool of Bethesda.

You parents and you families whose lives must be reordered because of a handicapped one, whose resources and time must be devoted to them, are special heroes. You are manifesting the works of God with every thought, with every gesture of tenderness and care you extend to the handicapped loved one. Never mind the tears nor the hours of regret and discouragement; never mind the times when you feel you cannot stand another day of what is required. You are living the principles of the gospel of Jesus Christ in exceptional purity. *And you perfect yourselves in the process.*

Now, in all of this there must be balance, for the handicapped have responsibility to work out their own salvation. The nearer the normal patterns of conduct and discipline apply to the handicapped, the happier they will be.

Every quarter of an inch of physical and mental improvement is worth striving for. The Prophet Joseph Smith said that "all the minds and spirits that God ever sent into the world are susceptible of enlargement" (*Teachings of the Prophet Joseph Smith,* sel. Joseph Fielding Smith [Salt Lake City: Deseret Book, 1967], p. 354).

I have known some who seemed to enjoy poor health and have unnecessarily interrupted the lives of those who were caring for them, making life miserable for all. They thrive on sympathy, which is generally very low in nourishment. To know just how far to press the handicapped when physical and emotional pain are involved may be the most difficult part for those who serve them. Nevertheless, as the Prophet Joseph Smith said, "There must be decision of character, aside from sympathy" (*History of the Church,* 4:570).

Think of this: Unless we die prematurely, every one of us may end up both physically and mentally handicapped. We would do well to make advance payments of service and compassion on which we may draw when that time comes.

Why not help the parents who have extra things to do and extra expenses and are confined because of a handicapped family member. Encourage the teachers and social workers who show such devotion to them. And it wouldn't hurt you to donate a few dollars or a few hours to one of the many organizations which help the handicapped. If we do this, without the slightest idea of selfishness, it will remain in our account against that time when we may need help. And the works of God will be made manifest in our lives.

"Ye cannot behold with your natural eyes, for the present time, the design of your God concerning those things which shall come hereafter, and the glory which shall follow after much tribulation.

"For after much tribulation come the blessings. Wherefore the day cometh that ye shall be crowned with much glory; the hour is not yet, but is nigh at hand." (D&C 58:3–4.)

I bear witness of the restoration which will come. Each body and mind will be restored in perfect frame. However long and unfair mortality may seem, however long the suffering and the waiting may be, He has said:

"After that cometh the day of my power; then shall the poor, the lame, and the blind, and the deaf, come in unto the marriage of the Lamb, and partake of the supper of the Lord, prepared for the great day to come.

"Behold, I, the Lord, have spoken it." (D&C 58:11–12.)

I am a witness of the condition of those who have gone beyond the veil, and we all have reason to glorify Him who is our Father and Him who is our Redeemer.

PART TWO

Priesthood

6

The Great Witness from These Conferences

PRESIDENT DAVID O. MCKAY INSTRUCTED the Church on the purposes for holding general conferences as follows:

"Reference to the Doctrine and Covenants will disclose the fact that there are four principal purposes for holding conferences of the Church:

"First, to transact current Church business.

"Second, to hear reports and general Church statistics.

"Third, to 'approve of those names which I (the Lord) have appointed, or to disapprove of them.'

"Fourth, to worship the Lord in sincerity and reverence, and to give and to receive encouragement, exhortation, and instruction." (In Conference Report, October 1938, pp. 130–31.)

The first conference was held on June 9, 1830. The minutes read:

> Our numbers were about thirty, besides whom many assembled with us, who were either believers or anxious to learn. Having opened by singing and prayer, we partook together of the emblems of the body and blood of our Lord Jesus Christ. We then proceeded to confirm several who had lately been baptized, after which we called out and ordained several to the various offices of the Priesthood. Much exhortation and instruction was given, and the Holy Ghost was poured out upon us in a miraculous manner—many of our number prophesied, whilst others had the heavens opened to their view. (*History of the Church,* 1:84–85.)

Address given at general conference October 1968.

This was the first conference of The Church of Jesus Christ of Latter-day Saints.

Seventeen years later there was held an even more humble conference than the first. It is described by Elder John Young.

> I reached the valley during the sitting of Conference, and some of the brethren said, "The Conference is sitting; won't you go?" So I walked down to where they were holding Conference, and I found them by the side of a haystack. There was Father John Smith and a little handful of men that might have been covered with a small tent, and they were holding the Semi-Annual Conference of the Church of Jesus Christ of Latter-day Saints. (*Journal of Discourses*, 6:232.)

Those men who met that October morning by that haystack had vision enough to know that someday their message would be carried across the world. From that small group of pioneers the influence of these great conferences has grown, and now the message is heard beyond the seas and across the world. There is a great spirit in general conferences.

President Heber J. Grant declared that:

"God established these conferences. Nothing but the spirit of the living God could bring together such a congregation. . . .

"The General Conferences of the Latter-day Saints are one of the great outstanding testimonies . . . of the divinity of the work in which we are engaged." (In Conference Report, October 1933, p. 118.)

What of those who attend conference? Perhaps we could introduce just one of them. Some time ago there came to a conference the religious editor of a large newspaper. He came across the country to get the "feel" of the conference.

Before the opening of a session, we came down the aisle of the building. It was filled to capacity. He noticed a middle-aged man, dressed unpretentiously, sitting next to the aisle, and asked to be introduced. We found him to be from the West Coast, a convert to the Church. As I recall, he had once been a member of the same church to which the editor belonged. He was a counselor in a bishopric. The interview proceeded something like this:

"How long have you been a member of the Church?"

"About eight years."

"Did you join the first time the missionaries contacted you?"

"Oh, no. It took me several weeks before I joined the Church." Then he added with a smile, "I don't like to rush into things."

"They tell me," the reporter inquired, "that the President of your Church is a prophet. Is that true?"

"Oh yes! I know him to be a prophet of God, just as much a prophet as any of the biblical prophets."

"Are you paid for your service in the Church?"

"Oh yes!" he said. "Generously paid—in blessings, not money. It seems that the principle of tithing requires that we pay for the privilege."

The editor, satisfied with the interview, turned to leave. Then, as an afterthought, he turned again with another question and said, "Tell me, why—why do you pay tithing?"

I noticed that the good brother's countenance became very serious, and there was a brimming bit of emotion in his eyes as he softly answered in a single word: "Obedience."

These, then, are those who come to conference. The lumberman from Oregon, the electrician from Maine, the policeman from Tonga, the nurseryman from Auckland, the civil servant from Holland.

There are those who saved and skimped to come. Others who come regard attendance at conference as an incidental expense.

And now of the men who speak here—the First Presidency, the Twelve Apostles, and the other General Authorities. They too come from varied occupations. One was a newspaper editor, another a building contractor, another an engineer. Several are attorneys. One was a bank president, another an airline executive, and two or three are insurance men. Several are teachers. Four of them hold doctorates. A number have held public office—two of them as cabinet members. Several have served in the military. They are all married men with families. Though most of them have known success in their chosen profession, almost to a man they come from humble beginnings.

As it was when He was here, they have been welded together in the ministry of the gospel of Jesus Christ. So it should be, for was not Peter a fisherman, and Andrew and James and John; and was not Matthew a publican?

What do General Authorities talk about in conference? Some people say that they are out of their province when they speak up on temporal or political issues. President John Taylor said of these conferences:

> As we possess bodies as well as spirits, and have to live by eating, drinking, and wearing, it becomes necessary that temporal matters should be considered and discussed in our Conferences, and that we should deliberate upon all things that are calculated to benefit, bless, and exalt the Saints of God, whether they refer to our spiritual affairs or to our avocations and duties in life as husbands and wives, as parents and children . . . whether they refer to the policy we should pursue in our commercial relations . . . or to any other matter affecting us as human beings composing part of the body politic of this nation or as citizens of the world (*Journal of Discourses*, 11:353–54).

Others complain that the Brethren are blind to social developments and urge them to be obedient to the "revelation of social progress."

Come the Sabbath day these men are scattered across the world holding conferences, bearing witness, and preaching the gospel. One will be in Hong Kong, another effecting a new organization in Australia or New Zealand. Others will be in South Africa, England, Germany, Canada, Brazil, or Guatemala.

Yet, when the council meetings come in the middle of the week, we find the Brethren here again. They sit in council to prayerfully deliberate over the affairs of the Church and kingdom of God here upon the earth.

Traveling as they do across the earth (literally, the full extent of it), it is hardly conceivable that they could miss or would ignore any significant development—social, political, religious, national, or racial—anywhere on the earth. Also, they have lifelong training and achievement in fields of activity so important to mankind.

However, it is not because of travel or professional success that we ought to pay heed to them. Nor is it because they are nimble of mind or wise in years. These things are incidental only.

We listen to them because they have been "called of God, by prophecy, and by the laying on of hands, by those who are in authority to preach the gospel and administer in the ordinances thereof" (Articles of Faith 1:5).

They are given divine authority. Not one of them aspired to the office he holds, nor did he call himself, for "in the Church of Jesus Christ of Latter-day Saints, one takes the place to which one is duly called," said President J. Reuben Clark, "which place one neither seeks or declines" (*Improvement Era,* June 1951, p. 412).

"Ye have not chosen me," said the Lord, "but I have chosen you, and ordained you" (John 15:16).

We don't have to listen to them or pay heed to them—we have our agency. But there is a lesson in scripture to consider.

The children of Israel entered the land of Edom. It was infested with serpents and snakes, the bite of which was so painful and so dangerous that they called them fiery, flying serpents. They cried for deliverance.

> And Moses prayed for the people.
> And the Lord said unto Moses, Make thee a fiery serpent, and set it upon a pole: and it shall come to pass, that every one that is bitten, when he looketh upon it, shall live.
> And Moses made a serpent of brass, and put it upon a pole, and it came to pass, that if a serpent had bitten any man, when he beheld the serpent of brass, he lived. (Numbers 21:7–9.)

"How silly," some must have said. "How can such a thing cure me? I'll not show my stupidity by paying any attention," and some would not look.

In First Nephi we read: "after they were bitten he prepared a way that they might be healed; and the labor which they had to perform was to look; and because of the simpleness of the way, or the easiness of it, there were many who perished" (1 Nephi 17:41).

The lesson is enlarged in the Gospel of John.

> And as Moses lifted up the serpent in the wilderness, even so must the Son of man be lifted up:
>
> That whosoever believeth in him should not perish, but have eternal life.
>
> For God so loved the world, that he gave his only begotten Son, that whosoever believeth in him should not perish, but have everlasting life. (John 3:14–16.)

And today many say, "How silly! How could accepting Christ save me?" They will not turn their heads to look nor incline their ears to hear. They ignore the great witness that comes from these conferences. We ought to, indeed we must, heed the counsel of these men, for the Lord said:

"What I the Lord have spoken, I have spoken, and I excuse not myself; and though the heavens and the earth pass away, my word shall not pass away, but shall all be fulfilled, whether by mine own voice or by the voice of my servants, it is the same.

"For behold, and lo, the Lord is God, and the Spirit beareth record, and the record is true, and the truth abideth forever and ever. Amen." (D&C 1:38–39.)

Though it is my privilege to serve among them, I have not forgotten for one moment that these men, the Brethren, are the servants of the Lord. And individually, independent of their knowing it, I know general conference is His voice speaking to His children.

7

The Twelve Apostles

IN THE COURSE OF ORGANIZING HIS CHURCH, Jesus "went out into a mountain to pray, and continued all night in prayer to God. And when it was day, he called unto him his disciples: and of them he chose twelve, whom also he named apostles." (Luke 6:12–13.) They were called from the ordinary paths of life.

Peter was the first called, and the Lord said to him, "I will give unto thee the keys of the kingdom of heaven: and whatsoever thou shalt bind on earth shall be bound in heaven: and whatsoever thou shalt loose on earth shall be loosed in heaven" (Matthew 16:19). This same sacred authority is inherent in the ordination of every Apostle.

Paul taught that the Apostles and prophets were called "for the perfecting of the saints, for the work of the ministry, for the edifying of the body of Christ," and he declared that these offices would endure "till we all come in the unity of the faith, and of the knowledge of the Son of God" (Ephesians 4:12–13).

THE APOSTASY AND THE RESTORATION

The Apostles in time were gone and, with them, the keys. Paul had prophesied of men being "carried about with every wind of doctrine" (Ephesians 4:14).

And so it was; instead of unity of faith, there came division and disunity.

Address given at general conference October 1996.

It was in this circumstance that young Joseph Smith prayed to know which of all the churches was true and which he should join.

Joseph's vision of the Father and the Son opened this dispensation. Then came the restoration of the fulness of the gospel of Jesus Christ with the same organization that existed in the primitive Church, built upon the foundation of Apostles and prophets (see Articles of Faith 1:6; Ephesians 2:20).

Some suppose that the organization was handed to the Prophet Joseph Smith like a set of plans and specifications for a building, with all of the details known at the beginning. But it did not come that way. Rather, it came a piece at a time as the Brethren were ready and as they inquired of God.

The Melchizedek Priesthood, the consummate authority given to man from God, was restored under the hands of Peter, James, and John. By them, the Lord said: "I have ordained you and confirmed you to be apostles, and especial witnesses of my name, and bear the keys of your ministry and of the same things which I revealed unto them; unto whom I have committed the keys of my kingdom, and a dispensation of the gospel for the last times" (D&C 27:12–13).

The First Presidency was in place by 1833; then two years later, in February of 1835, came the Quorum of the Twelve Apostles. And that is as it should be. The First Presidency came first in sequence and stands first in authority. And true to the pattern, it was made of men called from the ordinary pursuits of life.

APOSTLES ARE PROPHETS, SEERS, AND REVELATORS

With the First Presidency and the Quorum of the Twelve in place, with the offices of the Seventy and the Presiding Bishopric revealed, the proper order of things prevails. But there is a difference. Perhaps President J. Reuben Clark said it best:

> Some of the General Authorities [the Apostles] have had assigned to them a special calling; they possess a special gift; they are sustained as prophets, seers, and revelators, which gives them

a special spiritual endowment in connection with their teaching of [this] people. They have the right, the power, and the authority to declare the mind and will of God to his people, subject to the overall power and authority of the President of the Church. Others of the General Authorities are not given this special spiritual endowment . . . ; the resulting limitation . . . applies to every other officer and member of the Church, for none of them is spiritually endowed as a prophet, seer, and revelator. ("When Are Church Leader's Words Entitled to Claim of Scripture?" *Church News*, 31 July 1954, pp. 9–10.)

Furthermore, President Clark said that among those of the Twelve and the Presidency, "only the President of the Church, the Presiding High Priest, is sustained as Prophet, Seer, and Revelator for the Church, and he alone has the right to receive revelations for the Church, either new or amendatory, or to give authoritative interpretations of scriptures that shall be binding on the Church, or change in any way the existing doctrines of the Church" (*Church News*, 31 July 1954, p. 10).

It took a generation of asking and receiving before the order of things as we know it today was firmly in place. Each move to perfect that order has come about in response to a need and in answer to prayer. And that process continues in our day.

The Ministry of the Twelve

"The Twelve are a Traveling Presiding High Council, to officiate in the name of the Lord, under the direction of the Presidency of the Church, agreeable to the institution of heaven; to build up the church, and regulate all the affairs of the same in all nations" (D&C 107:33).

Where the First Presidency cannot go, the Twelve are sent "to unlock the door of the kingdom in all places" (D&C 112:17; see also D&C 107:35; 124:128). They are commissioned to go to all the world, for the word *Apostle* means "one [who is] sent forth" (LDS Bible Dictionary, "Apostle," p. 612).

"Wherefore," the Lord said, "in whatsoever place ye shall proclaim my name an effectual door shall be opened unto you, that they may receive my word" (D&C 112:19). And He promised, "Be thou humble; and the Lord thy God shall lead thee by the hand, and give thee answer to thy prayers" (D&C 112:10).

The Twelve Apostles "are called to be . . . special witnesses of the name of Christ in all the world" (D&C 107:23). Each carries that certain witness that Jesus is the Christ. President Joseph Fielding Smith taught that "every member of the Church should have the impressions on his soul made by the Holy Ghost that Jesus is the Son of God indelibly pictured so that they cannot be forgotten" ("The Twelve Apostles" [address to seminary and institute faculty, 18 June 1958], p. 6).

From Nephi we know that "angels speak by the power of the Holy Ghost" (2 Nephi 32:3). Mormon told us that "the office of their ministry is to call men unto repentance, and to fulfil and to do the work of the covenants of the Father, which he hath made unto the children of men, to prepare the way among the children of men." Mormon further explained that angels accomplish their ministry "by declaring the word of Christ unto the chosen vessels of the Lord, that they may bear testimony of him. And by so doing, the Lord God prepareth the way that the residue of men may have faith in Christ, that the Holy Ghost may have place in their hearts, according to the power thereof; and after this manner bringeth to pass the Father, the covenants which he hath made unto the children of men." (Moroni 7:31–32.)

APOSTLES HAVE THE GIFT OF DISCERNMENT

There is a power of discernment granted "unto such as God shall appoint . . . to watch over [His] church" (D&C 46:27). To discern means "to see."

President Harold B. Lee told me once of a conversation he had with Elder Charles A. Callis of the Quorum of the Twelve. Brother Callis had remarked that the gift of discernment was an awesome burden to carry. To see clearly what is ahead and yet find members slow to respond or resistant to counsel or even rejecting the witness of the Apostles and prophets brings deep sorrow.

Nevertheless, "the responsibility of leading this church" must rest upon us until "you shall appoint others to succeed you" (Declaration of the Twelve Apostles, reporting March 1844 meeting of the Twelve, Brigham Young Papers, Historical Department Archives, The Church of Jesus Christ of Latter-day Saints).

WARNING TO WRONGFUL CRITICS

The Lord warned us of those few in the Church "who have professed to know my name and have not known me, and have blasphemed against me in the midst of my house" (D&C 112:26).

"Thy voice," the Lord commanded the Twelve, "shall be a rebuke unto the transgressor; and at thy rebuke let the tongue of the slanderer cease its perverseness" (D&C 112:9).

Some few within the Church openly, or perhaps far worse in the darkness of anonymity, reproach their leaders in the wards and stakes and in the Church, seeking to make them "an offender for a word" (Isaiah 29:21; see also 2 Nephi 27:32), as Isaiah said. To them the Lord said:

> Cursed are all those that shall lift up the heel against mine anointed, saith the Lord, and cry they have sinned when they have not sinned . . . but have done that which was meet in mine eyes, and which I commanded them.
>
> But those who cry transgression do it because they are the servants of sin, and are the children of disobedience themselves. . . .
>
> . . . Because they have offended my little ones they shall be severed from the ordinances of mine house.
>
> Their basket shall not be full, their houses and their barns shall perish, and they themselves shall be despised by those that flattered them.
>
> They shall not have right to the priesthood, nor their posterity after them from generation to generation. (D&C 121:16–17, 19–21.)

That terrible penalty will not apply to those who try as best they can to live the gospel and sustain their leaders. Nor need it apply to those who in the past have been guilty of indifference or even opposition if they will repent, confess their transgressions, and forsake them (see D&C 58:43).

UNITY OF FIRST PRESIDENCY AND TWELVE

President Hinckley has reminded the Brethren that, while we are men called from the ordinary pursuits of life, there rests upon us a sacred ministry. And we take comfort in what the Lord said to the original Twelve: "Ye have not chosen me, but I have chosen you, and ordained you" (John 15:16).

While each feels his own limitation, there is strength in unity. Never in the history of the Church have the Brethren of the First Presidency and the Twelve been more united.

Each week we meet together in the temple. We open the meeting by kneeling in prayer, and we close with prayer. Every prayer is offered in the spirit of submission and obedience to Him who called us and whose servants and witnesses we are.

The Lord requires that "every decision made by either of these quorums must be by the unanimous voice of the same" and that "the decisions of these quorums . . . are to be made in all righteousness, in holiness, and lowliness of heart, meekness and long suffering, and in faith, and virtue, and knowledge, temperance, patience, godliness, brotherly kindness and charity" (D&C 107:27, 30). This we earnestly strive to do.

We know that we hold the power of the priesthood "in connection with all those who have received a dispensation at any time from the beginning of the creation" (D&C 112:31). We think of those who have preceded us in these sacred offices, and at times we feel their presence.

We are overcome with what the Lord said of those who hold these sacred callings: "Whatsoever they shall speak when moved upon by the Holy Ghost shall be scripture, shall be the will of the Lord, shall be the mind of the Lord, shall be the word of the Lord, shall be the voice of the Lord, and the power of God unto salvation" (D&C 68:4).

HEED THE COUNSEL OF THE LORD'S SERVANTS

During a very difficult time, the Lord gave the sternest warning that I know of in all scripture. It had to do with the building of the Nauvoo Temple. The Saints knew from experience that to proceed to build a temple would bring terrible persecution, so they delayed. The Lord extended the time and said, "If you do not these things at the end of the appointment ye shall be rejected as a church, with your dead, saith the Lord your God" (D&C 124:32).

Often overlooked in that revelation is a marvelous promise: "If my people will hearken unto my voice, and unto the voice of my servants whom I have appointed to lead my people, behold, verily I say unto you, they shall not be moved out of their place" (D&C 124:45).

Remember this promise; hold on to it. It should be a great comfort to those struggling to keep a family together in a society increasingly indifferent to, and even hostile toward, those standards which are essential to a happy family.

The promise is a restatement of what the Lord told the multitude: "Blessed are ye if ye shall give heed unto the words of these twelve whom I have chosen from among you to minister unto you, and to be your servants" (3 Nephi 12:1).

I repeat the promise that those who hearken to the voice of these men whom the Lord has raised up "shall not be moved out of their place" (D&C 124:45).

But the promise was followed with this caution: "But if they will not hearken to my voice, nor unto the voice of these men whom I have appointed, they shall not be blest" (D&C 124:46).

A SPECIAL WITNESS THAT JESUS IS THE CHRIST

The most precious thing we have to give is our witness of the Lord, our testimony of Jesus Christ.

I certify to you that the fourteen men with whom I share the ordination are indeed Apostles. In declaring this, I say no more than the Lord has taught, no more than may be revealed to anyone who seeks with a sincere heart and real intent for an individual witness of the Spirit.

These men are true servants of the Lord; give heed to their counsel. So, too, with the Seventy, who as especial witnesses carry an apostolic responsibility, and the Bishopric, worthy men of God. So, too, with the brethren and sisters across the world who are called to lead, who have earned that knowledge precious above all else.

There are limits to what the Spirit permits us to say (see Alma 12:9). And so I give my witness, my special witness, that Jesus is the Christ, that through a prophet-president He presides over this, "the only true and living church upon the face of the whole earth" (D&C 1:30).

8

"Come, All Ye Sons of God"

ONCE IN CANADA I STOOD BEFORE a group of missionaries impressed with how strong and clean missionaries are. Then I noticed an elder on the back row, worried and immature, hesitant and insecure in his calling. I had interviewed him earlier and had not helped him.

There came an inspiration, and I called him to my side and said, "Look at the missionaries and tell me what you see." He looked intently for a few moments, and I could feel that something was happening. Then I asked, "Did you ever know that before?" He shook his head; he had not known that before. "Will you be all right now?" I asked. He nodded his head yes, he would be all right. I then said, "Tell us what you see." He answered in one word. "Power!"

That is what I see and what I feel as I envision the brethren of the priesthood assembled across the world. I have great regard for the priesthood, and deep reverence for the ordinances we are authorized to perform. I feel an intense sense of obligation because, in addition to the opportunities which attend the priesthood, there are covenants connected with the ordinations we have received.

We who hold the priesthood of God are joined together by a sacred bond. We often speak of "holding" the priesthood. The word *hold* is most often used in connection with things that we can pick up and set down and then pick up again. We may, if we

---

From an address given 15 May 1983 at a Churchwide fireside commemorating the restoration of the priesthood.

are not properly taught, come to think of the priesthood in that way. The priesthood is not like that. It is an authority and a power that is a part of us.

We did not possess it when we came into mortality. But, if we honor it, we will keep it when we leave. We can hold it and at once share it. We can use the power of it to bless and nourish and protect our children. It is our duty to bless all of mankind.

I want to remind the young men about their priesthood duty. But first, I leave a brief message for the higher priesthood.

With the Melchizedek Priesthood, you are prepared, if you are worthy, to officiate in the ordinances of the gospel. Some ordinances are performed only in the holy temple. Those who receive them enter into covenants which carry the promise of supernal blessings.

If you have in any way broken your covenants, hasten to repent. If you have dishonored your priesthood through transgression, confess your sins and turn from them. The scriptures warn that no unclean thing can enter the presence of God.

The sacred ordinances of the temple are sometimes held up to open ridicule by enemies of the Church. Some foolish members take license from this and in an effort to defend the Church have been led to say more than is wise. Some, out of curiosity or claiming their interest is only academic or intellectual, presume to speak or to write about sacred ordinances.

In their speaking and writing they sometimes wade the muddy paths of opposition and apostasy. Then, without changing their boots, they seek to push open the doors of the temple and stride into those hallowed precincts to discuss the sacred ordinances.

In doing so they assume an authority that is not theirs. Do not be drawn to them. They say that they love the Church and that, in their own way, they are protecting it. They would do well to heed the voice of the Almighty as He commanded Moses: "Put off thy shoes from off thy feet, for the place whereon thou standest is holy ground" (Exodus 3:5).

How *should* we react when the sacred ordinances of the priesthood, of the temple, are held up to open public ridicule? What *should* we do in the face of the opposition that now confronts us? There is an answer in the Old Testament.

When the Israelites returned from captivity, they found Jerusalem destroyed. The prophet Nehemiah rallied the people to rebuild the wall about the city. Their enemies were amused. Sanballat mocked them and said, "Will they revive stones out of the heaps of rubbish?" Tobiah the Ammonite said, "Even that which they build, if a fox go up, he shall even break down their stone wall." (Nehemiah 4:2–3.)

But the wall went up, for "the people had a mind to work" (v. 6).

When the enemies saw that the wall was nearly up and that it was strong, they became worried. Sanballat and Geshem invited Nehemiah to meet with them in one of the villages in the plain of Ono. But Nehemiah said: "They thought to do me mischief. And I sent messengers unto them, saying, I am doing a great work, so that I cannot come down: why should the work cease, whilst I leave it, and come down to you?" (Vv. 2–3.) Their defense was simple and effective: "We made our prayer unto our God, and set a watch against them" (v. 9), and then went out to work.

And that is what we should do—go about our work, strengthen the wards and the stakes, the quorums and the families and the individual members. We have a work to do. Why should it cease while we do battle with our enemies? Brethren, set a watch and make a prayer and go about the work of the Lord. Do not be drawn away to respond to enemies. In a word, *ignore* them.

And now, for the message for the young men, we go back to the missionaries of whom I spoke in the beginning. There is a work for you to do as well, and it is your *duty* to do it.

That duty is proclaimed in the stirring anthem:

Come, all ye sons of God who have received the priesthood;
Go spread the gospel wide and gather in his people.
The latter-day work has begun, To gather scattered Israel in,
And bring them home to Zion to praise the Lamb.
(*Hymns*, no. 322.)

The message is repeated in the equally stirring lines:

> Ye elders of Israel, come join now with me
> And seek out the righteous, where'er they may be—
> In desert, on mountain, on land, or on sea—
> And bring them to Zion, the pure and the free.
> (*Hymns*, no. 319.)

Missionary service is the work of the Lord. We who hold the priesthood are the only ones on earth with authority to perform the ordinances connected with it. It is the duty of the young men holding the priesthood to serve in the mission field. In preparation for that service you need to do three things.

First, you should decide now, in spite of temptation or opposition, that you will serve a mission. It is your duty! Let me tell you of two young men who struggled with that decision.

The first was in premedical school. He had earned the attention of the faculty, who saw unusual potential in him. They fostered his medical career. But there was something in his way—a mission.

When finally he got the courage to speak about leaving school to serve a mission, his advisors became angry. They could not understand it. He had a medical ministry to perform. Let others preach. They would not let him do it. "If you do," he was told, "we will personally see that you are never admitted to this medical school, or to any other."

He went home to counsel with his father, who was a close friend of mine. What should he do? His father simply said, "Son, for twenty years your mother and I have tried to teach you your duty. If you have not learned in all of those years, how can I tell you in one weekend what you should do? This is a decision you must make yourself."

It was a terrible trial for him to decide, for in his mind he was choosing between becoming a doctor for his entire life or becoming a missionary for two years.

That young man is now a heart surgeon and a stake president. He is not old enough, really, to be either, but he is wise enough and inspired enough to succeed at both. The German language he learned on his mission helped him in school, the self-discipline he learned serves in his practice and in his life.

Another testimony came to him. When he returned to medical school, here and there the course was altered. But he received his specialist degree on the same schedule his advisors had planned before his mission. Oh, what a temptation! How near he came to making the mistake of his life. He is indebted to the Lord more than ever he was before.

The second young man faced a similar decision. He was a college athlete, the anchorman on his team. What about a mission? Should he drop out and risk losing that? Was not the fame of athletics a kind of mission in itself? He too went to his father, worried that perhaps a mission would be the end of his career in athletics. He had known of cases like that.

He too made the difficult decision—he would respond to his priesthood duty. During his mission he did not shoot one basket. When he returned, he started out as high-point man. Whether he wins honors in sports or not, he is already designated as a most valuable player on the Lord's team of priesthood bearers.

Now, it is possible that first young man might not have been admitted back into medical school, or the second would not have made the team. If that had happened, the Lord would surely have blessed them in other ways. But that is not the reason they served their mission—not for blessings! Not for the language, not to travel, not for the self-discipline. Each served a mission because it was his duty. It was not *his* mission, it was the *Lord's* mission.

Having made the decision, the second thing you must do is to remain worthy. In our society that will not be easy. But then why should it be easy? The physical strength of youth needs to be surpassed by the moral strength of your young manhood.

And you have the help of your teachers and leaders in the Church—and most of all your parents.

When Brother A. Theodore Tuttle was growing up, he became too interested at too early an age in a girlfriend. One morning after a late date, his mother sat with him on the porch swing and asked what time he had come in the night before. "Between nine and ten," he replied. He had marked a 9 on one side of the front door and a 10 on the other. He always came in between 9 and 10.

His mother then talked very seriously of duty, of a mission, and of priesthood responsibility. She counseled him wisely and firmly. One can only imagine where he would be if his mother had not intruded that much into his affairs at that moment—or if he had resented it.

What of the young man who has already stumbled, who has already made the type of mistake that can disqualify one from serving a mission. I challenge you, I especially challenge you, to prepare for your mission. Pick yourself up and dust yourself off. It will be harder than you know. But it will be possible. Where is your young manhood? Use the cleansing power of your priesthood. Go to your bishop. It is your duty to go—your duty! He will help you erase a sad episode from your life. We need you! We have the world to teach and warn. We have the world to convert. The Lord really needs you.

Finally, you need to prepare financially. Every one of you should have a savings account specifically reserved for your mission. I speak to that young man who does not have any idea how he can finance a mission. I do not know either. But I do know this: if you have faith and determine that you will go, there will be a way. Opportunities will come to you as manna from heaven. Do not let that deter you from your duty.

Young brethren, a mission is a duty—it is *your* duty. It will cost you something—certainly money, and certainly years of your life, possibly much, much more.

I once held the hand of a tall, handsome college basketball star as he drew his last breath, dead from a disease he had contracted while serving the Lord in a foreign land. A casualty? Perhaps. A winner? Wait and we will see. He answered the call. He will not, in the eternal scheme of things, be granted less than he might have earned had he lived a very long life. For he answered the call to duty, priesthood duty.

Some young men are—now I must choose the right word— forced? persuaded? encouraged? compelled? to serve a mission by a sweet girl. She flashes her pretty eyelashes and says with some determination that she will one day marry one who has served an honorable mission.

It is interesting indeed what inspires spiritual patriotism. How quickly a young hero will line up to enlist with that kind of en- couragement. God bless the sisters who have such power to re- cruit missionaries.

Some elders find themselves in the mission field and do not quite know how they got there, and wonder, are they really quali- fied or are they there in some measure under false pretenses? Was it only to please his parents? That is all right. For while they may go on a mission for a superficial reason, they stay on their mission for the right reason. They may go out of *duty*, but they stay out of *devotion*. For, on the mission, there comes an individual testimony of the gospel.

If you have been handicapped by some accident of nature or by disease or disability, perhaps you may want to go on a mission. But you cannot serve a regular mission because of a wheelchair, or a brace, or a tongue or eyes or ears that will not respond properly.

You can serve a different type of a mission, one which in your case is equally approved by the Lord. Perhaps a stake mission, perhaps not that—but the Lord loves you and will bless you for your desire and compensate you in other ways. You can at least be an example of *wanting to go*. You can inspire, or shame, some in- decisive youth who has the physical capacity to serve a mission but who does not want to go.

I am sure there are some who have not served a mission. Per- haps you did not really understand. Perhaps your decision for one reason or another was that you could not go. Perhaps you were not in the Church at that age. Some missed their mission because of military service.

Whatever the reason, there is no time to brood over that now.

Every member is a missionary. Devote attention to encouraging and financing and preparing your children and others to serve on missions. Many dreams are realized through our children. The time may come when you may go as a missionary couple.

Look forward, not backward. Magnify your priesthood.

Missionary work is a priesthood duty. Go ye therefore and preach the gospel to every nation, kindred, tongue, and people, and the Lord will bless you and build you up, for the gospel of Jesus Christ is true. The message that we preach is true. I bear witness of this, that we are presided over by a prophet, that Jesus is the Christ, that God is our Father, and as we serve Him we do our priesthood duty.

PART THREE

Learning

9

The Gospel—
The Foundation for Our Career

THERE IS A RECURRING THEME IN THE revelations having to do with learning. And, from the beginning, Church leaders have counseled us to get all of the education we can as a preparation for and as an improvement of our careers. For example: "Seek ye diligently and teach one another words of wisdom; yea, seek ye out of the best books words of wisdom; seek learning, even by *study* and also by *faith*" (D&C 88:118; emphasis added; see also D&C 90:15; 109:7).

Learning is to be accompanied by faith, and as the Book of Mormon teaches us, learning "is good if [we] hearken unto the counsels of God" (2 Nephi 9:29).

There is one thought that must come at the very beginning of a discussion on occupations and careers in order to establish it as preeminent, and it is this:

Do not ever belittle anyone, including yourself, nor count them, or you, a failure, if your livelihood has been modest. Do not ever look down on those who labor in occupations of lower income. There is great dignity and worth in any honest occupation. Do not use the word *menial* for any labor that improves the world or the people who live in it.

There is no shame in any honorable work, and the principle of faith, which the Lord connected with learning, is precious above the technologies of man.

There will be many who struggle through life with small ownership and low income who discover, because they have been decent,

---

Address given at general conference April 1982.

the meaning of the scripture, "He that is greatest among you," let him be "the least and the servant of all" (Matthew 23:11; D&C 50:26).

While schooling and education generally go together, there are kinds of wisdom which are not usually taught in school class-rooms. To illustrate, I begin with the Old Testament record of Naaman who, as the commander of the armies of Syria, had "given deliverance" to his country. He became a leper and the king of Syria feared he would die.

An Israelite slave girl who served Naaman's wife spoke of prophets in Israel who had the power to heal.

The king of Syria sent a message to the king of Israel saying, "I have sent Naaman my servant to thee, that thou mayest recover him of his leprosy." The king of Israel suspected a plot and com-plained, "He seeketh a quarrel against me. . . . Am I God, to kill and to make alive, that this man doth send unto me to recover a man of his leprosy?"

Elisha, the prophet, heard of the king's distress. And "he sent to the king, saying, . . . let him come now to me." Elisha would heal Naaman, and he told why: that "he shall know that there is a prophet in Israel."

When Naaman was near, Elisha sent a messenger to him, say-ing, "Go and wash in Jordan seven times, . . . and "thou shalt be clean." Naaman was angry. There were rivers aplenty in Syria, as good, he thought, as the Jordan. He had expected Elisha to per-form some impressive ceremony like clapping his hands upon him. And he "turned . . . away in a rage."

But one of his servants (it seems there is always a servant) courageously chastised the general and said, "If the prophet had bid thee do some *great* thing, wouldest thou not have done it?"

Humbled by his servant, Naaman "went . . . down, and dipped himself seven times in Jordan, according to the saying of the man of God: and he was clean." (2 Kings 5:1–14; emphasis added.)

Human nature hasn't changed over the years. Even today some of us expect to be bidden to do some "great things" in order to receive the blessings of the Lord. When we receive ordinary counsel on ordinary things, there is disappointment, and, like Naaman, we turn away.

Let me give you a modern-day example. In many conference sermons President Spencer W. Kimball included at least a sentence telling us to clean up, paint up, and fix up our property. Many of us have paid little attention to the counsel.

Question: Why would a prophet tell us to do that? Has he no great prophecies to utter?

But, is that not a form of prophecy? For has he not said to us over and over again, "Take good care of your material possessions, for the day will come when they will be difficult, if not impossible, to replace."

Already there is a fulfillment. Families who might have afforded a home when first he spoke now despair of getting one.

For some reason, we expect to hear, particularly in welfare sessions, some ominous great predictions of calamities to come. Instead, we hear quiet counsel on ordinary things which, if followed, will protect us in times of great calamity.

It was Alma the prophet who said, "By small and simple things are great things brought to pass; and small means in many instances doth confound the wise" (Alma 37:6).

Now, all of this was to prepare you for the fact that the counsel I will give may seem ordinary, even trivial to some of you. But it will be consistent with the doctrines and principles announced by the First Presidency when the welfare program was first introduced:

> Our primary purpose [is] to set up, in so far as it might be possible, a system under which the curse of idleness would be done away with, the evils of a dole abolished, and independence, industry, thrift and self-respect be once more established amongst our people. The aim of the Church is to help the people to help themselves. Work is to be re-enthroned as the ruling principle of the lives of our Church membership. (In Conference Report, October 1936, p. 3.)

That emphasis, on self-reliance, suggests something about education. We cannot expect the Church to assume responsibility for the schooling of all of us.

One of the questions most often asked of General Authorities as we travel usually begins in this way: "Why doesn't the Church . . . ?" And then there follows a description of some worthy project that would, if it should succeed, bring credit to the Church and benefit many people.

For example, why doesn't the Church establish schools to prepare members for financial security?

Some years ago I was near our front gate splitting rails for a fence. A young man came to make a delivery. He had recently returned from overseas combat duty. He had falsified his age and left school to join the Marines. When I asked about his future plans, he didn't know. Jobs were scarce; he had no skills to offer.

I counseled him to go back to high school and get his diploma. He thought he couldn't do that; he was too old now. "If you do it," I told him, "you probably will not exactly fit in. And the students will call you the 'old man' or 'grandpa.' But you faced an enemy in combat; surely you've got the courage to face that."

The lesson is this. I only spent ten minutes with him, sitting on a log by our front gate. I did not build a school or ask the Church to build one. I did not pay his tuition or prepare his lessons. What he needed was some direction, some counsel, some encouragement, and some vision. In this case he took the counsel and returned to school. Now he has a family and an occupation.

I only gave him vision and encouragement. It does not take additional Church budget to do that. That is the responsible role of every priesthood leader in counseling members on careers. We must help people to help themselves.

Several years ago a certain country was emerging from a long period of political and economic distress, and there was a need for skilled workers of many kinds. Some of our local leaders, sensing the need, conceived the idea of establishing vocational schools in our chapels to train the brethren in their skills. They could then upgrade themselves in their employment. It was a very appealing idea.

They pointed out that the money expended would be justified on the basis that these brethren would return in tithes more than the cost of the program. They were greatly disappointed when the Brethren did not approve their idea.

There were several things they'd not considered. The most important was that vocational training was already available to those who *really* looked for it. Classes to train new employees, and to upgrade the experienced ones, were offered by business and industry, and by their government.

What our brethren needed most was counsel and encouragement to take advantage of opportunities that were already available.

We ourselves are responsible to seek out and take advantage of every opportunity to improve ourselves.

Now, there are some things that the Church *must* do, for we are commanded to do them. We must preach the gospel. We must build temples. We must perfect the Saints. These things others cannot do. The many other good things (which are not central to the mission of the Church) must take second place. For we do not have the resources to do all that is worth doing, however worthy it may be.

While we cannot build schools for everyone, there is a most important contribution the Church *can* make to our careers, one that is central to the mission of the Church. And that is to teach moral and spiritual values.

There are ordinary virtues which influence our careers even more than technical training; among them are these:

- Integrity
- Dependability
- Courtesy
- Respect for others
- Respect for property

Let me illustrate one or two of these.

It is likely that our children, and yours, for the first part of their married life at least, will live in rented apartments.

I had a conversation with a stake president who owns a large number of apartments which he rents to middle-income families. As he showed them to me, he described the abuse of his property—not just the normal wear and tear, but outright abuse bordering on vandalism.

Such conduct is unworthy of a Latter-day Saint! We should know better than that. We should be willing to drive a nail or set a screw in a hinge, if it's needed.

Our people should regard an apartment as their home and keep it inviting and clean and in good repair. Has not the prophet told us to do it? When they leave an apartment, it should be clean and essentially ready for the next tenant.

Now, what has this got to do with a career? Surely you can see the transfer of learning from our homes to our work.

Years ago my father, as a young married man with several children, went nervously into the bank in Brigham City to ask for a loan to start in business. He was asked about collateral. He had none beyond his willingness to work and some mechanical aptitude.

The banker, in turning down his request, happened to ask father where he lived. "In the old box house on First West," was the answer. The banker passed that corner on the way to work. He'd watched the transformation in the yard. He'd wondered who lived there, and admired what they were doing.

Father got the loan to start in business on the strength of the flowers that mother had planted in the yard of a very modest adobe house they were renting.

My wife and I have raised a large family on a very modest income, and it's likely that our children are going to have the same privilege. In order to prepare them, we've trained them to do ordinary, necessary things as preparation for their careers.

For instance, we have maintained an area (sometimes it's the corner of a basement room) where there is a workbench, where projects could be left. There can be some paint or a little sawdust on the floor, without a problem. In spite of continuous cleanup, this area is perpetually untidy, but with a purpose.

We have followed another practice. Each Christmas, at least one of the presents for the boys has been a hand tool. When they were old enough, a good metal toolbox was included. When each has left home, he has had his own set of tools and some knowledge of how to use them. He can tune up a car, or drive a nail, or turn a screw, or replace a plug or a faucet washer.

The girls, in turn, have learned to cook and to sew, and each has left home with a sewing machine. This training is doubly important—first, in frugal living at home, and then in their value as an employee. They would, we hoped, be not only good, but good for something.

Now, I have an idea that some soul will be very upset with us for not providing our boys with a sewing machine and our girls a box of tools as well.

So I hasten to explain that our boys can cook enough to survive a mission and they can sew on a button. The girls in turn can change a faucet washer and drive a nail, and both of them can type and even change a tire on a car.

While many, many occupations suit a man or a woman equally well, I, for one, have grave concern over the growing trend for both men and women to choose careers which in some respects are against their very natures.

We have tried to prepare our boys for manly work and our girls for work that would suit the opportunities that womanhood will bring them. In defense of our doing that, I can only observe that in this Church we are not exempt from using common sense.

There are so few nowadays who are really willing to work. We must train our children and ourselves to give, in work, the equivalent of the pay we receive and perhaps just a little extra.

There are so few who will come a bit early to get organized for the day, or stay a minute after to tidy up the workbench or the desk for tomorrow's work.

The attitude that demands compensation and benefits in excess of the value of labor has come near destroying the economy of the world. Now, however, many workers quite willingly accept reductions in pay just to keep their jobs. That spirit of doing a little extra would have prevented the crisis had it been evident earlier.

Family responsibilities and tight budgets sometimes prevent us from obtaining all the schooling we desire.

We can, however, improve ourselves. The only tuition required is the time it takes, the work required, and the desire to build into our lives the ordinary virtues so much in demand and so short in supply.

I hope you have not been too disappointed that I have not presented some "great thing" for you to do, some elaborate formula for career planning, rather than such ordinary things so obvious, so close to us, that they are often overlooked.

There is a formula. The Lord said: "Verily I say unto you, that every man who is obliged to provide for his own family, let him provide, and he shall in nowise lose his crown; *and let him labor in the church*" (D&C 75:28; emphasis added).

The gospel of Jesus Christ is the formula for success. Every principle of the gospel, when lived, has a positive influence over your choice of an occupation and on what you will achieve. The counsel to labor in the Church has great value. Living the gospel will give you a perspective and an inspiration that will see you successful however ordinary your work may be or however ordinary your life may seem to others.

God bless the members of this Church, that you can be happy with who you are and where you are, that you can improve yourselves. We pray that God will bless those who are struggling now with unemployment, with the loss of their employment, with the fear of that loss. May He bless us that we can build into our lives those principles of reliance and integrity that have been part of the gospel from the very beginning, for the gospel is true.

10

"To Be Learned Is Good If . . ."

WE ARE COUNSELED TO "SEEK . . . diligently and teach one another words of wisdom; yea, seek ye out of the best books words of wisdom; seek learning, even by study and also by faith" (D&C 88:118).

The words *study* and *faith* each portray a type of education. First, we are commanded to "teach one another the *doctrine* of the kingdom. Teach ye diligently and my grace shall attend you, that you may be instructed more perfectly in theory, in principle, in doctrine, in the law of the gospel, in all things that pertain unto the kingdom of God." (D&C 88:77–78.)

And we are also "to obtain a knowledge of history, and of countries, and of kingdoms, of laws of God and man, and all this for the salvation of Zion" (D&C 93:53; see also 88:79).

The Church must concentrate on moral and spiritual education; we may encourage secular education but not necessarily provide it.

THE SPIRIT OF GATHERING

There is much said in the scriptures about the gathering of the Saints. In the early days, the call went out to converts all over the world to gather to Zion. And they came, first as a trickle, and then as a stream. The Zion to which they came was under terrible persecution and was greatly strengthened by their very numbers.

Because there were no public schools, the Church opened

Address given at general conference October 1992.

schools. Even in our own generation, schools have been established where there were none.

Something of the spirit of gathering touched our schools. I can remember, as supervisor of seminaries, attending stake conferences with the General Authorities to recruit students for our Church schools.

In an area conference held in Mexico City in 1972, Elder Bruce R. McConkie said:

> [The] revealed words speak of . . . there being congregations of . . . covenant people of the Lord *in every nation, speaking every tongue,* and *among every people* when the Lord comes again. . . .
>
> The place of gathering for the Mexican Saints is in Mexico; the place of gathering for the Guatemalan Saints is in Guatemala; the place of gathering for the Brazilian Saints is in Brazil; and so it goes throughout the length and breadth of the whole earth. . . . Every nation is the gathering place for its own people. (Mexico and Central America Area Conference, 26 August 1972, p. 45.)

The following April, President Harold B. Lee quoted those words in general conference and, in effect, announced that the pioneering phase of gathering was now over. The gathering is now to be out of the world into the Church in every nation. (See Conference Report, April 1973, p. 7.)

As public schools became available, most of the Church schools were closed. At once, seminaries and institutes of religion were established in many nations.

Some few schools are left over from that pioneering period, Brigham Young University and Ricks College among them.

Now BYU is full to the brim and running over. It serves an ever-decreasing percentage of our college-age youth at an ever-increasing cost per student. Every year a larger number of qualified students must be turned away simply because there is no room for them.

Leaders and members plead for us to duplicate these schools elsewhere. But we cannot, neither should we, attempt to provide secular education for all members of the Church worldwide. Our youth have no choice but to attend other schools.

Those who cannot attend Church schools have been counseled by the First Presidency to gather where there is an institute of religion. The institute program will be greatly enhanced for your benefit.

Some of you live in countries where schooling is relatively easy to obtain. Others must struggle simply to learn to read and to write because schools, or the means to attend them, are beyond your reach.

Some of you require special education because of learning disabilities or limitations in what you can hear or see or how you can move about.

For many it is a matter of money. The economic condition of your family or your country makes getting an education seem like an impossible dream.

NO RESPECTER OF PERSONS

You who find schooling easily available must remember this: "God is no respecter of persons: but in every nation he that feareth him, and worketh righteousness, is accepted with him" (Acts 10:34–35; see also Moroni 8:12; D&C 1:35; 38:16).

The Lord does not, and the Church cannot, admit to favoritism toward those who are able to obtain professional degrees as compared to those who seek training in a practical field or those who have little or no schooling at all.

Unless you have the vision of the ever-growing millions of members all over the world, you may not understand why the Brethren make the decisions we make concerning Church schools.

THE END OF A TRADITION

Several years ago at a family reunion, Sister Packer and I announced the end of a family tradition. Our ten children and some of our grandchildren have attended BYU. It will not be possible for all of our grandchildren to follow that tradition.

We advised them to follow the counsel of the Brethren. If they cannot attend a Church school, and this will be increasingly the case, they should gather with other members of the Church at a school where an institute of religion is available to them. Then, as they study secular subjects, they may learn the "covenants and church articles" as the scriptures tell us we should (see D&C 42:13).

They will not be judged on how many degrees they hold or how extensive their schooling may be, but on how well educated they are in those things which are of eternal value.

We told our family that we will be quite as proud of them learning a trade as we would a profession. We will be equally pleased with them if they choose vocational schools and make their living with their hands.

After all, education continues as long as we live. If there is ever an end to secular learning, surely there is no end to spiritual learning.

The Lord's work moves forward on the strength of those who labor in the workaday world: the apprentice, artisan, journeyman, laborer, office worker, waitress—and, in a class by itself, homemaker.

A WARNING

We must not ignore these warnings in the Book of Mormon: "The people began to be distinguished by ranks, according to their riches and their chances for learning; yea, some were ignorant because of their poverty, and others did receive great learning because of their riches. Some were lifted up in pride, and others were exceedingly humble. . . . And thus there became a great inequality . . . , insomuch that the church began to be broken up." (3 Nephi 6:12–14.)

Jacob warned us of those who "when they are learned they think they are wise, and they hearken not unto the counsel of

Because of such quality teachers, our schools can be unsurpassed in meeting the standards set by those who accredit schools, yet unique in mission, and contribute much to the Church even though a growing number of eligible students cannot enroll.

Because salaries of faculty and staff are paid from the tithes of the Church, there is a standard for them as well. A Church university is not established to provide employment for a faculty, and the personal scholarly research is not a dominant reason for funding a university.

The educational Mt. Everest mentioned by President Kimball will not be achieved solely through the prominence of the faculty (see *Church News,* 22 November 1980, p. 4). It will be reached through the achievement of the students.

THE PURPOSE

Our purpose is to produce students who have that rare and precious combination of a superb secular education, complemented by faith in the Lord, a knowledge of the doctrines He has revealed, and a testimony that they are true.

For those very few whose focus is secular and who feel restrained as students or as teachers in such an environment, there are at present in the United States and Canada alone over 3,500 colleges and universities where they may find the kind of freedom they value. And we are determined to honor the trust of the tithe payers of the Church.

Students at other schools soon learn that some professors deliberately undermine faith and challenge your moral and spiritual values. You in turn must be free, even in our own schools, to return that challenge and defend your right to believe in God, to keep the covenants you have made through baptism and which you renew through the sacrament.

God, for they set it aside, supposing they know of themselves, wherefore, their wisdom is foolishness and it profiteth them not. And they shall perish." He added: "But to be learned is good *if* they hearken unto the counsels of God." (2 Nephi 9:28–29; emphasis added.)

A Second Tuition

For those privileged to attend a Church school, there is a tuition other than money which we must require of you—a tuition of conduct and performance. Students who enroll in Church schools do so after an interview with their bishop and with their stake president. They must commit to a standard of conduct consistent with faithful Church membership.

Occasionally a bishop will interview one who easily qualifies scholastically but who has not kept the standards of the Church. Perhaps the bishop will reason: "The atmosphere at a Church school will reform this one." Bishops should not do that. It is not fair to the literally thousands who are totally faithful but must be turned away because there is no room.

And if, while enrolled, a student is found to be transgressing, or in violation of standards pledged at the time of enrollment, however hard it may be upon the bishop, the student, or the parents, continued enrollment at a Church school must be called into question.

Dedicated Faculty

Our faculties and staff are a miracle—men and women who have the highest academic degrees, many of them having been acclaimed for outstanding achievement. They are at once men and women of humility and faith.

We are grateful for teachers who will challenge students to high scholarship but would not even think of undermining testimony or acting in any way subversive to the progress of the Church and kingdom of God.

A Dream Worth Pursuing

We encourage our youth in every country to get an education. Even if at times it seems hopeless. With determination and faith in the Lord, you will be blessed with success. It is a dream well worth pursuing.

On one occasion, I spent a few minutes with a young man who had left high school and entered the military. Now he was trying to decide what to do with his life. I encouraged him to return to finish high school.

I did not provide him with money; the Church had no school for him, not even a scholarship. In those few minutes, I simply taught him that self-reliance which is such a part of our way of life. Even though overage, he returned to finish high school, and now he provides for his family and encourages his children in their search for truth.

Follow the Leaders

A verse from the Doctrine and Covenants is relevant to the subject of the gathering: "I say unto you, that it shall not be given to any one to go forth to preach my gospel, or to build up my church, except he be ordained by some one who has authority, and it is known to the church that he has authority and has been regularly ordained by the heads of the church" (D&C 42:11).

There are some among us now who have not been regularly ordained by the heads of the Church who tell of impending political and economic chaos, the end of the world—something of the "sky is falling, chicken licken" of the fables. They are misleading members to gather to colonies or cults.

Those deceivers say that the Brethren do not know what is going on in the world or that the Brethren approve of their teaching but do not wish to speak of it over the pulpit. Neither is true. The Brethren, by virtue of traveling constantly everywhere on earth, certainly know what is going on, and by virtue of prophetic insight are able to read the signs of the times.

Do not be deceived by them—those deceivers. If there is to be any gathering, it will be announced by those who have been regularly ordained and who are known to the Church to have authority.

Come away from any others. Follow your leaders who have been duly ordained and have been publicly sustained, and you will not be led astray.

The Lord said:

> The glory of God is intelligence, or, in other words, light and truth.
>
> Light and truth forsake that evil one. . . .
>
> I have commanded you to bring up your children in light and truth. (D&C 93:36–37, 40.)

God grant that as a church and as families and as individuals we can bring up our children, our youth, in light and truth and that they may receive the testimony of Him of whom we bear witness—our Redeemer, our Savior, even Jesus Christ.

11

Language of the Spirit

SEVERAL YEARS AGO I WAS ASSIGNED TO go to Germany to take care of some important Church business. As I looked forward to that assignment, I worried a great deal. I knew there would be some very important interviews and that I do not speak German. I knew that most of those with whom I would conduct the Church business did not speak English. I felt helpless.

After taking care of some work in English for about two weeks, I was finally on the plane to Germany. As I sat there pondering and praying, the voice of the Lord came into my mind, and gave me some instructions. You know, the Lord doesn't speak in either English or German, and He can speak pure intelligence into our minds without passage of time. The message was something like this: "What are you worried about? There is another language, the language of the Spirit. Those brethren will know that language. You know the language. There will be no problem." I was greatly comforted. And I had a great experience on that occasion.

As a witness that there is that universal language, the language of the Spirit, since then I have never been very anxious when I have had to go into other countries. Sometimes we will visit among people of seven or eight languages on one trip. But always there is that language of the Spirit.

In the first section of the Doctrine and Covenants the Lord gave this instruction: "The voice of warning shall be unto all people, by the mouths of my disciples, whom I have chosen in these last

From an address given 7 August 1976 at Dortmund, Germany, area conference.

days . . . for I . . . have commanded them" (D&C 1:4–5). And the Lord has said that this is a day of warning, not a day of many words.

I am reminded of a story of a man who awakened in a hotel room one cold winter night. He had been very happy to reach his hotel to be sheltered from the cold weather. Sometime in the night he heard a woman in the next room calling, "Hans, Hans, get up!" He turned over in bed and went to sleep. Then he heard the woman again calling to her husband, "Hans, Hans, get up! The hotel is on fire! The hotel is on fire!" This time he sat up and he could smell smoke. He quickly slipped on a robe and ran to the stairway, down the stairs, and opened the door. Then a blast of cold air and snow hit him. He stopped for a moment and then said to himself, "My name isn't Hans." And he went back up to bed.

The next morning his body was found in the charred ruins of the hotel. Because his name wasn't Hans. Now the voice of warning is to all people. And what I have to say, I would like to say to you.

We have the tendency sometimes when we hear a sermon to say, "It is too bad that Brother Jacobs isn't here; he needs that lesson." Or, "It is too bad Sister Muller isn't here; she sure needed that." Now the voice of warning is to all people.

Let me speak of an important event that we have had in the Church. Not too far from Church headquarters, in Idaho, there was a great tragedy. A great earthwork dam collapsed. There were seventeen miles of water backed up in the canyon behind the dam. All of that was loosed on the valley below.

It was a beautiful, quiet, sunny Saturday morning. Just below in the valley were two or three little communities—7,800 people in all. A few miles farther down the valley were another 25,000 to 30,000 people, almost all of them Latter-day Saints. All were going about their work, getting ready for Sunday.

The first place the water hit was the Wilford Ward area. That area was washed away, all of it: all of the houses, all of the barns, all of the fences. The ward chapel was completely destroyed. The ward was gone, just like that.

Then the water hit Sugar City. The same thing happened. Sugar City was gone. The stake center stood and a few of the houses, but they were terribly damaged. The water broke into the wall of the stake center and picked up all of the benches and just tore the inside of the building out. Then it broke out the other wall and went on its way.

In all, 790 homes were destroyed. Many of them vanished without a trace. In some places you could see a cement foundation. Another 800 homes and many businesses and churches and schools were badly damaged.

Now you are wondering about the people, about the 25,000 Latter-day Saints, all in the face of this flood that Saturday morning. Very few died by drowning. Only six. That is a miracle. An expert said that 5,300 should have perished.

But only six died by drowning. How could that be? They couldn't just run upstairs and get on the roof and be safe, because the houses were washed away. They couldn't just run up on the hill—most of them had several miles to go before they reached safety. Then how were they saved?

There was a warning. It was only a short one. Some of the people only had a few minutes. But there was a warning. And Latter-day Saints pay attention to warnings. If we are living righteously, we are easily warned. And so, the word went out just before noon that the dam was beginning to crumble. Those who heard obeyed the scripture. Let me read another verse or two from the Doctrine and Covenants.

"Behold, I sent you out to testify and warn the people, and it becometh every man who hath been warned to warn his neighbor" (D&C 88:81).

And that is what happened in Idaho. Some of the people heard, and they began to warn their neighbors. Now how did they do that? Call them on the telephone? "It's a beautiful day today, a nice day for a ride. Do you think you would like to go over to Rexburg sometime this afternoon and visit the college? It's up on the hill. Oh, you are too busy. Well, you think about it, and I'll call later this afternoon."

No! no! That isn't the way it was! If they got them on the phone they didn't speak, they screamed: "The dam is breaking! Get your children! Get to high ground!" They ran from neighbor to neighbor. And they knocked on the door, and if no one would open, they kicked the door down or smashed in the window to warn them.

Only six drowned. What about them? One was a fisherman just below the dam. He had no warning. Two people heard the warning but didn't believe it. They were found in their car, but they had moved too late. Three others heard the warning but went back to get some of their possessions. Latter-day Saints pay attention to warnings.

There are pages of miracles that took place individually. One young man was in town when he heard the warning. He knew that his parents were not at home out on the farm, but his little sister was there, and she was sick in bed. When it was all over, she had been saved.

One father was at the college in Rexburg doing some work that Saturday morning. Someone knocked on his door and said: "Turn on your radio; I've heard that the dam is breaking." He thought of his wife and the boys out irrigating on the farm. And he had the car. There was no time for him to go. When it was all over with, his wife and his children were there with him, warned and rescued by the neighbors.

Now there is a great message in this. You have heard the Brethren speak about testimony, about our obligations to share the gospel. Sometimes we are just polite; we talk to someone like this:

"Would you like to hear something about the gospel?"

"No, thank you, I'm too busy."

"All right, good-bye."

And that's that. They are drowned in the flood of evil, subject to the second death, which is the spiritual death, which is separation from the presence of our Heavenly Father.

Now, the Lord has said that in His Church and kingdom there is safety and that we will be protected. That is the only place on earth where this protection is. And it behooves every man and every woman and every child who has been warned to warn his neighbors. We can do this in two ways: First, we can live the gospel completely, live it religiously.

I had a missionary in Denmark ask a question: "I am striving for perfection. Some of the other missionaries say, 'You are foolish; you can't really be perfect.' What do you believe?"

I said I believe the scriptures: "Be ye therefore perfect, even as your Father which is in heaven is perfect" (Matthew 5:48). And then I humbly admitted that I was perfect in some things. Now, I am perfect when it comes to never touching tobacco—never. Alcohol—never. Tea, coffee—never. I am perfect there. Now, there are many things where I am not perfect yet. But I *am* perfect when it comes to not committing murder. I have never done that. I will never do that. We can be perfect, a little bit at a time, always perfecting ourselves, becoming Latter-day Saints. In living that way we warn our neighbors.

Second, we can strive for perfection in being missionaries. And if we are not perfect in all things, at least we can seriously heed the warnings that are given.

I bear witness that God lives, that Jesus is the Christ—I know that. The other churches teach that He is but an influence somewhere in the far reaches of the heavens. We know Him to be Jesus Christ, the Son of God. We know that He has a body of flesh and bones, that He presides over the Church, that He directs it through His earthly prophet, that there are Apostles upon the earth who are witnesses of Him, special witnesses who move about the earth raising a voice of warning and bearing witness of Him.

12

Personal Revelation:
The Gift, the Test, and the Promise

I REACH OUT TO THE YOUTH OF THE CHURCH who now face "perilous times," as the Apostle Paul prophesied would come in the last days (see 2 Timothy 3:1).

In order to prepare you, and protect you, I will tell you, as plainly as I can, what I have learned about personal revelation.

DUAL BEINGS

There are two parts to your nature—your temporal body born of mortal parents, and your immortal spirit within. You are a son or daughter of God.

Physically you can see with eyes and hear with ears and touch and feel and learn. Through your intellect, you learn most of what you know about the world in which we live.

But if you learn by reason only, you will never understand the Spirit and how it works—regardless of how much you learn about other things.

The scriptures teach that "great men are not always wise" (Job 32:9). Spiritually you may "know not, and know not that you know not," and be "ever learning, and never able to come to the knowledge of the truth" (2 Timothy 3:7).

Your spirit learns in a different way than does your intellect.

For "there is a spirit in man: and the inspiration of the Almighty giveth them understanding" (Job 32:8), and the Spirit of

---

Address given at general conference October 1994.

Christ "giveth light to every man that cometh into the world" (D&C 84:46).

I will use the words *see, hear,* and *feel* to teach about revelation, but I will use them as they are used in the scriptures.

THE GIFT OF THE HOLY GHOST

Following baptism, in the ordinance of confirmation, you received the *gift* of the Holy Ghost.

While the Holy Ghost may inspire all mankind, the gift carries the right to have it as a "constant companion" (D&C 121:46). It is "by the power of the Holy Ghost [that you] may know the truth of all things" (Moroni 10:5; see also 2 Nephi 32:5).

We are told that "angels speak by the power of the Holy Ghost" (2 Nephi 32:3). We are even told that when we speak by the power of the Holy Ghost, we "speak with the tongue [or in the same language] of angels" (2 Nephi 31:13; 32:2).

PRAYER

You have your agency, and inspiration does not—perhaps cannot—flow unless you ask for it, or someone asks for you.

No message in scripture is repeated more often than the invitation, even the command, to pray—to ask.

Prayer is so essential a part of revelation that without it the veil may remain closed to you. Learn to pray. Pray often. Pray in your mind, in your heart. Pray on your knees.

BEGIN WHERE YOU ARE

You must begin where you are. Pray, even if you are like the prophet Alma when he was young and wayward, or if you are like Amulek, of the closed mind, who "knew concerning these things, yet . . . would not know" (Alma 10:6).

Prayer is *your* personal key to heaven. The lock is on your side of the veil (see Revelation 3:20).

STUDY

But that is not all. To one who thought that revelation would flow without effort, the Lord said:

"You have not understood; you have supposed that I would give it unto you, when you took no thought save it was to ask me.

"But, behold, I say unto you, that you must study it out in your *mind*; then you must ask me if it be right, and if it is right I will cause that your bosom shall burn within you; therefore, you shall *feel* that it is right." (D&C 9:7–8; emphasis added.)

This burning in the bosom is not purely a physical sensation. It is more like a warm light shining within your being.

Describing the promptings from the Holy Ghost to one who has not had them is very difficult. Such promptings are personal and strictly private! (See 1 Nephi 14:28–30; 2 Nephi 32:7; Alma 12:9–11.)

STILL SMALL VOICE

The Holy Ghost speaks with a voice that you *feel* more than you *hear.* It is described as a "still small voice" (D&C 85:6). And while we speak of "listening" to the whisperings of the Spirit, most often one describes a spiritual prompting by saying, "I had a *feeling* . . ."

The Prophet Joseph Smith explained:

A person may profit by noticing the first intimation of the spirit of revelation; for instance, when you feel pure intelligence flowing into you, it may give you sudden strokes of ideas, so that by noticing it, you may find it fulfilled the same day or soon; . . . those things that were presented unto your minds by the Spirit of God, will come to pass; and thus by learning the Spirit of God and understanding it, you may grow into the principle of revelation, until you become perfect in Christ Jesus (*Teachings of the Prophet Joseph Smith,* sel. Joseph Fielding Smith [Salt Lake City: Deseret Book Co., 1938], p. 151).

Revelation comes as words we *feel* more than *hear.* Nephi told his wayward brothers, who had been visited by an angel, "Ye were past *feeling,* that ye could not *feel* his words" (1 Nephi 17:45; emphasis added).

The scriptures are full of such expressions as "The veil was taken from our minds, and the eyes of our understanding were opened" (D&C 110:1), or "I will tell you in your mind and in your heart" (D&C 8:2), or "I did enlighten thy mind" (D&C 6:15), or "Speak the thoughts that I shall put into your hearts" (D&C 100:5). There are hundreds of verses that teach of revelation.

President Marion G. Romney, quoting the prophet Enos, said, "While I was thus struggling in the spirit, behold, the voice of the Lord came into my mind" (Enos 1:10). Enos then related what the Lord put into his mind.

"This," President Romney said, "is a very common means of revelation. It comes into one's mind in words and sentences. With this medium of revelation I am personally well acquainted." (In Conference Report, April 1964, p. 124.)

We do not seek spectacular experiences. President Spencer W. Kimball spoke of the many who "have no ear for spiritual messages . . . when they come in common dress. . . . Expecting the spectacular, one may not be fully alerted to the constant flow of revealed communication." (*The Teachings of Spencer W. Kimball,* ed. Edward L. Kimball [Salt Lake City: Bookcraft, 1982], p. 457.)

PROMPTING

This voice of the Spirit speaks gently, prompting you what to do or what to say, or it may caution or warn you. Ignore or disobey these promptings and the Spirit will leave you. It is your choice—your agency.

FAITH

The flow of revelation depends on your faith. You exercise faith by causing, or by making, your mind to accept or believe as truth that which *you* cannot, by reason alone, prove for certainty (see Alma 32:27–28, 38).

The first exercising of your faith should be your acceptance of Christ and His atonement.

As you test gospel principles by believing without knowing, the Spirit will begin to teach you. Gradually your faith will be replaced with knowledge.

You will be able to discern, or to *see,* with spiritual eyes.

Be believing and your faith will be constantly replenished, your knowledge of the truth increased, and your testimony of the Redeemer, of the Resurrection, of the Restoration will be as "a well of living water, springing up unto everlasting life" (D&C 63:23; see also John 4:14; Jeremiah 2:13). You may then receive guidance on practical decisions in everyday life.

WORD OF WISDOM

Your body is the instrument of your mind. In your emotions, the spirit and the body come closest to being one. What you learn spiritually depends, to a degree, on how you treat your body. That is why the Word of Wisdom (see D&C 89) is so important.

The habit-forming substances prohibited by that revelation—tea, coffee, liquor, tobacco—interfere with the delicate feelings of spiritual communication, just as other addictive drugs will do.

Do not ignore the Word of Wisdom, for that may cost you the "great treasures of knowledge, even hidden treasures" (D&C 89:19) promised to those who keep it. And good health is an added blessing.

MUSIC

Make wholesome music of all kinds a part of your life.

Then learn what *sacred* music has to do with revelation. The Lord said, "My soul delighteth in the song of the *heart;* yea, the song of the righteous is a prayer unto me, and it shall be answered with a blessing upon their heads" (D&C 25:12; emphasis added).

Secular music may be inspiring in a classical or popular sense, but it will not prepare your mind to be instructed by the Spirit as will sacred music.

The Apostle Paul counseled the Ephesians to "be filled with the Spirit; *speaking* to *yourselves* in psalms and hymns and spiritual songs, singing and making melody *in your heart* to the Lord" (Ephesians 5:18–19; emphasis added).

REVERENCE

Prelude music, reverently played, is nourishment for the spirit. It invites inspiration. That is a time to, as the poet said: "Go to your bosom . . . and ask your heart what it doth know" (William Shakespeare, *Measure for Measure,* act 2, scene 2, lines 136–37). Do not ever disturb prelude music for others, for reverence is essential to revelation. "Be still," He said, "and know that I am God" (Psalm 46:10).

Now a warning! Some music is spiritually very destructive. You young people know what kind that is. The tempo, the sounds, and the lifestyle of those who perform it repel the Spirit. It is far more dangerous than you may suppose, for it can smother your spiritual senses.

TEMPTATION

Now, young people, pay attention! Before I say another word about personal revelation, I must tell you so that you cannot possibly misunderstand: "There are many spirits which are false spirits" (D&C 50:2; see also v. 3). There can be counterfeit revelations, promptings from the devil, temptations! As long as you live, in one way or another the adversary will try to lead you astray. "For after this manner doth the devil work, for he persuadeth no man to do good, no, not one; neither do his angels; neither do they who subject themselves unto him" (Moroni 7:17).

The Prophet Joseph Smith said that "nothing is a greater injury to the children of men than to be under the influence of a false spirit when they think they have the Spirit of God" (*Teachings of the Prophet Joseph Smith,* p. 205).

The seventh chapter of Moroni in the Book of Mormon tells you how to test spiritual promptings. Read it carefully—over and over.

By trial, and some error, you will learn to heed these promptings.

If ever you receive a prompting to do something that makes you *feel* uneasy, something you know in your *mind* to be wrong and contrary to the principles of righteousness, do not respond to it!

THE CHURCH

The Lord reveals His will through dreams and visions, visitations, through angels, through His own voice, and through the voice of His servants. "Whether by mine own voice," He said, "or by the voice of my servants, it is the same" (D&C 1:38).

The Lord's house is a house of order. The Prophet Joseph Smith taught that "it is contrary to the economy of God for any member of the Church, or any one [else], to receive instruction for those in authority, higher than themselves" (*Teachings of the Prophet Joseph Smith,* p. 21).

You may receive revelation individually, as a parent for your family, or for those for whom you are responsible as a leader or teacher, having been properly called and set apart.

If one becomes critical and harbors negative feelings, the Spirit will withdraw. Only when they repent will the Spirit return. My experience is that the channels of inspiration always follow that order. You are safe following your leaders.

THE COMFORTER

Now, do not suppose that you will be spared from sorrow, disappointment, failure, fear. These come to all. They are essential to our testing.

When sore trials come, you will learn why the Holy Ghost is called the Comforter.

You must face life "led by the Spirit, not knowing beforehand the things which [you] should do," (1 Nephi 4:6) just as Nephi did.

You may not yet have a certain witness that Jesus is the Christ. Exercise your faith and trust in those who do.

I have that certain witness. It came to me in my youth. During those early periods of doubt, I leaned on the testimony of a seminary teacher. Although I did not know, somehow I *knew* that he *knew*.

The Lord said:

> If ye love me, keep my commandments.
>
> And I will pray the Father, and he shall give you another Comforter, that he may abide with you for ever;
>
> Even the Spirit of truth; whom the world cannot receive, because it seeth him not, neither knoweth him: but ye know him; for he dwelleth with you, and shall be in you.
>
> I will not leave you comfortless: I will come to you. (John 14:15–18.)

I bear witness of the power of the Spirit and thank God that this incomparable gift is given to you to guide you as you move forward to a happy life.

13

Gifts of the Spirit

Author's note: Since this was presented more as a classroom presentation than as a sermon, I am including in this printed version the full text of some scriptures referred to but not quoted completely.

I KNOW FULL WELL THAT YOU ARE students. I wonder if you would fancy that I am a teacher so that I might make my presentation perhaps a little differently than usual.

I begin with section 46 of the Doctrine and Covenants, verse 2. It will outline what we can comply with as related to meetings and to the Spirit: "But notwithstanding those things which are written, it always has been given to the elders of my church from the beginning, and ever shall be, to conduct all meetings as they are directed and guided by the Holy Spirit" (D&C 46:2).

Section 46 is a special section. The subject of that section is the gifts of the Spirit, and that is our subject. The gifts of the Spirit are sacred, and I approach this subject with reverence, for we are counseled in the scriptures that we should not speak lightly of sacred things.

WHAT ARE THE GIFTS OF THE SPIRIT?

There are three quite comprehensive listings of these gifts in the scriptures—interestingly enough, one each in the Bible, the Book of Mormon, and the Doctrine and Covenants. I would like

Address given at Brigham Young University 16-stake fireside 4 January 1987.

to just skip through them, touching on a word or phrase here and there, hoping that you will see the similarities and understand something of the words that are emphasized.

From the Bible:

> Now there are *diversities of gifts,* but the *same Spirit.*
> And there are *differences of administrations,* but the *same Lord.*
> And there are diversities of operations, but it is the same God which worketh all in all.
> But the manifestation of the Spirit is given *to every man to profit withal.* (1 Corinthians 12:4–7; emphasis added.)

Now we know two things: (1) that there is a diversity of gifts of the Spirit and (2) that they are given to all men to profit withal. The verses that follow mention the gifts of the word of wisdom, the word of knowledge, of faith, healing, working of miracles, prophecy, and other gifts:

> For to one is given by the Spirit the *word of wisdom;* to another the *word of knowledge* by the same Spirit;
> To another *faith* by the same Spirit; to another the *gifts of healing* by the same Spirit:
> To another the *working of miracles;* to another *prophecy;* to another *discerning of spirits;* to another *divers kinds of tongues;* to another the *interpretation of tongues:*
> But all these worketh that one and the selfsame Spirit, dividing to every man severally as he will.
> For as the body is one, and hath many members, and all the members of that one body, being many, are one body: so also is Christ. (1 Corinthians 12:8–12; emphasis added.)

From the Book of Mormon:

> And again, I exhort you, my brethren, that ye deny not the gifts of God, for *they are many;* and they come from the *same God.*

And there are *different ways* that these gifts are administered;
but it is the same God who worketh all in all; and they are given
by the manifestations of the Spirit of God unto men, to profit
them.

For behold, to one is given by the Spirit of God, that he may
teach the word of wisdom;

And to another, that he may *teach the word of knowledge* by
the same Spirit;

And to another, *exceedingly great faith;* and to another, the
gifts of healing by the same Spirit;

And again, to another, that he may *work mighty miracles;*

And again, to another, that he may *prophesy* concerning all
things;

And again, to another, the *beholding of angels and ministering
spirits;*

And again, to another, *all kinds of tongues;*

And again, to another, the *interpretation of languages* and of
divers kinds of tongues.

And then this very significant verse:

And all these gifts come by the Spirit of Christ; and they
come unto *every man* severally, according as he will. [I take the
word *he* to refer to us, meaning that the gifts will be received as
we will.]

And then Moroni said:

And I would exhort you, my beloved brethren, that ye remember that every good gift cometh of Christ. (Moroni 10:8–18;
emphasis added.)

From Doctrine and Covenants section 46:

And again, verily I say unto you, I would that ye should always remember, and always retain in your minds what those gifts
are, that are given unto the church.

For all have not every gift given unto them; for there are *many gifts,* and to *every man* is given a gift by the Spirit of God.

To some is given one, and to some is given another, that all may be profited thereby.

To some it is given *by the Holy Ghost* to know *that Jesus Christ is the Son of God,* and that he was crucified for the sins of the world.

To others it is given to *believe on their words,* that they also might have eternal life if they continue faithful.

And again, to some it is given by the Holy Ghost *to know the differences of administration,* as it will be pleasing unto the same Lord, according as the Lord will, suiting his mercies according to the conditions of the children of men.

And again, it is given by the Holy Ghost to some to *know the diversities of operations,* whether they be of God, that the manifestations of the Spirit may be given to *every man* to profit withal.

And again, verily I say unto you, to some is given, by the Spirit of God, the *word of wisdom.*

To another is given the *word of knowledge,* that all may be taught to be wise and to have knowledge.

And again, to some it is given *to have faith to be healed;*

And to others it is given to have *faith to heal.*

And again, to some is given the *working of miracles;*

And to others it is given *to prophesy;*

And to others the *discerning of spirits.*

And again, it is given to some to *speak with tongues;*

And to another is given the *interpretation of tongues.*

And all these gifts come from God, for the benefit of the children of God. (D&C 46:10–26; emphasis added.)

There are several other verses and then:

He that asketh in the Spirit asketh according to the will of God; wherefore it is done even as he asketh (v. 30).

Unto the Bishop and Elders

Then after admonishing us to give thanks to God for the blessings that we receive, section 46 closes with these verses:

And unto the bishop of the church, and unto such as God shall appoint and ordain to watch over the church and to be elders unto the church, are to have it given unto them *to discern all those gifts* lest there shall be any among you professing and yet be not of God.

And it shall come to pass that he that asketh in Spirit shall receive in Spirit;

That unto some it may be given to have *all those gifts,* that there may be a head [I take that to refer to the prophet, who is the head of the Church], in order that every member may be profited thereby.

He that asketh in the Spirit asketh according to the will of God; wherefore it is done even as he asketh.

And again, I say unto you, all things must be done in the name of Christ, whatsoever you do in the Spirit;

And ye must give thanks unto God in the Spirit for whatsoever blessing ye are blessed with.

And ye must practise virtue and holiness before me continually. Even so. Amen. (Vv. 27–33; emphasis added.)

The Gifts Are Diverse

Now, you notice that in all three of these listings there is harmony—each one mentions the *diversity of gifts,* but the *same Spirit.*

I list again those listed in these three citations, plus other references in the scriptures (and there are many of them), among which gifts are:
- Faith
- The gift of prophecy
- The gift of administration
- Seeing as seers see

- Revelation
- Discernment
- Visions
- Dreams
- Visitations
- Promptings
- Feelings
- Sensing whether a decision is right or wrong
- Gift of healing
- Warnings
- Raising the dead
- Gift of tongues
- Gift of interpretation of tongues
- Gift of translation
- The gift to teach by the Spirit

There is another gift, a little difficult to describe, but I think we could say that it is the gift to be guided, or the gift of guidance—difficult to define, but I think you know what I mean. When certain events happen (often small events in our lives) that could not possibly be coincidental, we get the impression that there is a Power and a Source that knew we would be there and what we would be about. Examples of this happen often in genealogical work when things just seem to come together, and in many other aspects of our lives these spiritual gifts come.

These gifts have always been in the Church, and Alma spoke of the care we must take and of the responsibility that is ours because these gifts are with us.

Quoting Alma, we make another listing:

Having been visited by the Spirit of God;
having conversed with angels, and
having been spoken unto by the voice of the Lord; and
having the spirit of prophecy,
and the spirit of revelation,
and also many gifts,
the gift of speaking with tongues,

and the gift of preaching,
and the gift of the Holy Ghost,
and the gift of translation; . . .

And now behold I say unto you, that if this people, who have received so many blessings from the hand of the Lord, should transgress contrary to the light and knowledge which they do have, I say unto you that if this be the case, that if they should fall into transgression, it would be far more tolerable for the Lamanites than for them (Alma 9:21, 23).

If we know what the Lamanites were like in that day, we know that Alma was issuing a warning.

GIFT

I must emphasize that the word *gift* is of great significance, for a gift may not be demanded or it ceases to be a gift. It may only be accepted when proffered.

Inasmuch as spiritual gifts are gifts, the conditions under which we may receive them are established by Him who offers them to us. Spiritual gifts cannot be forced, for a gift is a gift. They cannot, I repeat, be forced, nor bought, nor earned in the sense that we make some gesture in payment and expect them to automatically be delivered on our own terms.

There are those who seek such gifts with such persistence that each act moves them farther from them. And in that persistence and determination they place themselves in spiritual danger. Rather, we are to live to be worthy of the gifts, and they will come according to the will of the Lord.

Brigham Young said something in his day that surely applies to ours:

There is no doubt, if a person lives according to the revelations given to God's people, he may have the Spirit of the Lord to signify to him his will, and to guide and to direct him in the discharge of his duties, in his temporal as well as his spiritual exercises. I am satisfied, however, that in this respect, we live far beneath our privileges. (*Discourses of Brigham Young*, ed. John A. Widtsoe [Salt Lake City: Bookcraft, 1998], p. 32.)

Spiritual gifts belong to the Church, and their existence is one of the great and abiding testimonies of the truth of the gospel. They really are not optional with the Church. Moroni taught that if they were absent, then "awful is the state of man" (Moroni 7:38).

We are to seek to be worthy to receive these gifts according to the way that the Lord has directed.

Now, I say that again—we are to seek for spiritual gifts in the Lord's way.

WE ARE TO SEEK FOR SPIRITUAL GIFTS

Paul wrote to the Corinthians: "Now concerning spiritual gifts, brethren, I would not have you ignorant" (1 Corinthians 12:1).

There are many, many other references, and I will just touch on them here and there.

And again I would exhort you that ye would come unto Christ, and lay hold upon every good gift, and touch not the evil gift, nor the unclean thing (Moroni 10:30).

Another:

But covet earnestly the best gifts (1 Corinthians 12:31).

I define *covet* in that frame of reference as "ardently desire in a righteous way."

Then:

Follow after charity, and desire spiritual gifts (1 Corinthians 14:1).

Charity, as defined by Mormon, is "the pure love of Christ" (Moroni 7:47). Usually we get the wrong direction on that—we think the pure love of Christ would be a marvelous thing for us to receive, and hardly ever do we realize that it is an obligation that we are to give. But read that properly: "Follow after charity, and desire spiritual gifts."

Another:

> Even so ye, forasmuch as ye are zealous of spiritual gifts, seek that ye may excel to the edifying of the church (1 Corinthians 14:12).

I have already referred to verse 2 of section 46 of the Doctrine and Covenants about the instruction to conduct all meetings as we are directed by the Spirit—it was given to the elders in the beginning and "ever shall be":

> But notwithstanding those things which are written, it always has been given to the elders of my church from the beginning, and ever shall be, to conduct all meetings as they are *directed and guided by the Holy Spirit* (D&C 46:2; emphasis added).

A verse in Moroni in the Book of Mormon says the same thing:

> And their meetings were conducted by the church after the manner of the workings of the Spirit, and by the power of the Holy Ghost; for as the power of the Holy Ghost led them whether to *preach,* or to *exhort,* or to *pray,* or to *supplicate,* or to *sing,* even so it was done (Moroni 6:9; emphasis added).

SIGNS TO FOLLOW THE BELIEVERS

The signs will follow those that believe. That is another theme in scripture that is almost everywhere:

And [Jesus] said unto them, Go ye into all the world, and preach the gospel to every creature.

He that believeth and is baptized shall be saved; but he that believeth not shall be damned.

And these signs shall follow them that believe; In my name shall they cast out devils; they shall speak with new tongues;

They shall take up serpents; and if they drink any deadly thing, it shall not hurt them: they shall lay hands on the sick, and they shall recover. (Mark 16:15–18.)

And, skipping several others, observe this: "Verily, verily, I say unto you, He that believeth on me, the works that I do shall he do also; and greater works than these shall he do; because I go unto my Father" (John 14:12).

WE ARE NOT TO SEEK AFTER SIGNS: A DEFINITION OF TERMS

So we have the assignment to seek after spiritual gifts. Then we have the very clear notice that signs will follow those that believe. The scriptural direction that we should seek after spiritual gifts and that these signs would follow those that believe has a very important counterbalance, for by warnings that are unmistakable we are not to seek after the signs.

I would like to give something of a definition of my own of the two terms—*spiritual gifts* and *signs*.

A spiritual gift is an endowment of spiritual power: For example, the gift of faith or the gift of discernment, neither of which may be visible.

Signs, on the other hand, are evidences of visible manifestations that a spiritual power is present: visible miracles, such as healing a person or raising one from the dead.

The scriptures make it clear that we are not to seek after signs, and many references explain that spiritual gifts, and the signs which follow them, are a product of faith and that faith is not an outgrowth of the signs. Let me repeat that. Spiritual gifts and the signs that follow them are the product of faith and not the reverse—faith is not an outgrowth of the signs. If we misunderstand this, surely we will place ourselves in spiritual jeopardy. In four places in the Bible and various other places, there is this very clear statement:

"An evil and adulterous generation seeketh after a sign; and there shall no sign be given to it, but the sign of the prophet Jonas" (Matthew 12:39; see also 16:4; Luke 11:29).

Now from the Doctrine and Covenants:

> And he that seeketh signs shall see signs, but not unto salvation.
>
> Verily, I say unto you, there are those among you who seek signs, and there have been such even from the beginning;
>
> But, behold, faith cometh not by signs, but signs follow those that believe.
>
> Yea, signs come by faith, not by the will of men, nor as they please, but by the will of God. (D&C 63:7–10.)

The Lord said:

> Wherefore, I, the Lord, am not pleased with those among you who have sought after signs and wonders for faith, and not for the good of men unto my glory (v. 12).

BE NOT DECEIVED

We speak often of angels and visitations, and we should keep in mind that Moroni taught that there are angels of the adversary. There are forty-six references in the scriptures to evil or unclean spirits. So we must stay spiritually attuned, as attested by Moroni.

> Wherefore, beware lest ye are deceived: and that ye may not be deceived seek ye earnestly the best gifts, always remembering for what they are given (D&C 46:8).

But ye are commanded in all things to ask of God, who giveth liberally; and that which the Spirit testifies unto you even so I would that ye should do in all holiness of heart, walking uprightly before me, considering the end of your salvation, doing all things with prayer and thanksgiving, that ye may not be seduced by evil spirits, or doctrines of devils, or the commandments of men; for some are of men, and others of devils (D&C 46:7).

Occasionally we will find someone who claims to receive spiritual revelations. One of the evidences of false revelation that you had better be careful of is that individuals begin to include others as though they are receiving spiritual instruction for others. They seem to think somehow that the inspiration they receive supersedes that which the bishops or stake presidents might receive and comes from some higher source than these brethren are privileged to have.

Some are deceived, and endless mischief occurs and sorrow results. The destructive result of these who are misled is twofold. One of the problems is that thereafter many become afraid, themselves thinking that they might be misled or go too far. And then they hold back and submerge the spiritual part of their lives. Then, for fear of going too far, they avoid the very spiritual feelings that can lead them and make them worthy to receive these gifts.

If we are not well grounded in spiritual matters, we tend to draw back and lose trust and faith. When that happens, the Church is weakened and the progress of the work is affected. Remember faith is the one essential prerequisite to receive the spiritual gifts.

Now, there is one way to protect ourselves from this. The key is given to us in section 46. This is a verse of vital importance. "And unto the bishop of the church, and unto such as God shall appoint and ordain to watch over the church and to be elders unto the church, are to have it given unto them to discern all those gifts lest there shall be any among you professing and yet be not of God" (v. 27).

And skipping a verse:

> That unto some it may be given to have all those gifts, that
> there may be a head, in order that every member may be profited
> thereby (v. 29).

That, of course, refers to the prophet and President of the
Church, who has the right and authority to exercise all of the keys
and is able to receive all of those gifts that there might "be a head,
in order that every member may be profited thereby."

The key is to follow the counsel of your bishop and those elders who are ordained to watch over the Church. Then you will
be safe. And if someone pretends to be receiving revelations that
include you, that would be a spiritual gift that does not come from
the right source. Flee from that with all speed.

There is great purpose in teaching the lines of authority and
the patterns of protocol in priesthood government. Sometimes
members get a little weary of that, but there is a great and powerful protection there.

Protection is embodied in that very unpopular word (particularly when we are young)—*obedience!* We need to understand the
order of the priesthood and the safety in following the counsel of
priesthood leaders. Then if someone should try to mislead us, our
bishop or stake president can counsel us and, if we have the right
spirit, we will obediently follow and all will be well with us.

I have not known of any case where members who have been
misled would not have been protected had they followed the counsel of their bishop. Invariably they had received counsel but turned
aside from it thinking that their inspiration took precedence. I repeat, there is great protection in following the counsel of our local
leaders if we are interested in qualifying for spiritual gifts.

SPIRITUAL GIFTS ARE A PRODUCT OF FAITH

Spiritual gifts, I repeat, are a product of our faith, and if we do
not have them, something is less than it should be. Consider this
prophecy of Mormon's:

And now, my beloved brethren, if this be the case that these things are true [and he is talking about miracles and faith] which I have spoken unto you, and God will show unto you, with power and great glory at the last day, that they are true, and if they are true has the day of miracles ceased? [Did you notice that he said "the last day"?]

Or have angels ceased to appear unto the children of men? Or has he withheld the power of the Holy Ghost from them? Or will he, so long as time shall last, or the earth shall stand, or there shall be one man upon the face thereof to be saved?

Behold I say unto you, Nay; for it is by faith that miracles are wrought; and it is by faith that angels appear and minister unto men; [and then this warning] wherefore, if these things have ceased wo be unto the children of men, for it is because of unbelief, and all is vain.

For no man can be saved, according to the words of Christ, save they shall have faith in his name; wherefore, if these things have ceased, then has faith ceased also; and awful is the state of man, for they are as though there had been no redemption made. (Moroni 7:35–38.)

Do you remember the comment that he who *will* not read has no advantage over him who *cannot* read.

If . . . faith has ceased also; . . . awful is the state of man, for they are as though there had been no redemption made (v. 38).

Mormon was an optimist because he concluded with this: "But behold, my beloved brethren, I judge better things of you, for I judge that ye have faith in Christ because of your meekness; for if ye have not faith in him then ye are not fit to be numbered among the people of his church" (v. 39).

Well, those things are with us. We do not talk about them often or lightly.

Mormon explains the special responsibility of those who are called to positions of leadership in the Church, the chosen vessels of the Lord. He says:

Have miracles ceased? Behold I say unto you, Nay; neither have angels ceased to minister unto the children of men.

For behold, they [meaning the angels] are subject unto him, to minister according to the word of his command, showing themselves unto them of strong faith and a firm mind in every form of godliness. (Vv. 29–30.)

He then tells us what the office of an angel is:

And the office of their ministry is to call men unto repentance, and to fulfill and to do the work of the covenants of the Father, which he hath made unto the children of men, to prepare the way among the children of men (v. 31).

Then he says how they are to do it: "by declaring the word of Christ unto the chosen vessels of the Lord, that they may bear testimony of him" (v. 31).

Now, you would do well, you in your youth, to learn to heed the counsel and the testimonies of the chosen vessels of the Lord.

And by so doing [Mormon continues], the Lord God prepareth the way that the residue of men may have faith in Christ, that the Holy Ghost may have place in their hearts, according to the power thereof; and after this manner bringeth to pass the Father, the covenants which he hath made unto the children of men (v. 32).

SPIRITUAL GIFTS DO NOT COME AUTOMATICALLY

Spiritual gifts do not come lightly or easily. There are other gifts that we could comment upon. One of them is referred to (I mention reverently) in such simple terms as "Blessed are the pure in heart: for they shall see God" (Matthew 5:8).

And in that verse from section 93:

Verily, thus saith the Lord: It shall come to pass that every soul who forsaketh his sins and cometh unto me, and calleth on

my name, and obeyeth my voice, and keepeth my commandments, *shall see my face and know that I am* (v. 1; emphasis added).

And then section 88 brings back that same parameter:

> Therefore, sanctify yourselves that your minds become single
> to God, and the days will come that you will see him; for he will
> unveil his face unto you, and it shall be in his own time, and in
> his own way, and according to his own will (v. 68).

Well, there is much more that could be said. I have looked
through the scriptures, looking for those things that are deterrents
to the reception of spiritual gifts. Of course, transgression and
wickedness are obvious. They short-circuit the possibility of receiving spiritual gifts. Apathy and indifference, being caught up
too much in the things of the world, are two others.

RELYING TOO MUCH ON ONE'S INTELLECT

And then there is the matter that you ought to have somewhere in your consciousness in a university setting—and that is,
we can rely too much on our intellects, on our minds. Now our
"thinkers" are necessary and we need to use them, but we need to
learn to *feel* a few things.

Do you remember that lesson the Lord taught when Oliver
Cowdery was trying to translate, and he thought it would just be
given to him. The Lord said, in effect, "You didn't use your mind
first; you didn't use your intellect first. You were to study it out,
and then the spiritual element would be there." (See D&C 9:7–9.)

We are to keep those sensitive feelings as a part of our lives.

You remember the incident in 1 Nephi where Laman and
Lemuel had been abusing Nephi unmercifully. And Nephi said in
effect, "I can't understand you":

> Ye are swift to do iniquity but slow to remember the Lord
> your God. Ye have seen an angel, and he spake unto you; yea, ye
> have heard his voice from time to time; and he hath spoken unto

you in a still small voice, but ye were past *feeling,* that ye could not *feel* his words. (1 Nephi 17:45; emphasis added.)

SPIRITUAL GIFTS CARRY GREAT RESPONSIBILITY

Spiritual gifts carry great responsibility, and we are not to talk about them lightly. I see no purpose, for instance, in chattering endlessly about evil spirits. Missionaries somehow are wont to do that, and returned missionaries are not exempt from it. There is no purpose in it. I would not do it, and I would not stay where it is done. Do not sit around and talk about the so-called experiences of those who have confronted evil spirits.

I have always had the idea that one's deep spiritual experiences are very personal and very private. Sometimes people have wondered why the Brethren do not talk more about their spiritual experiences, and some have assumed that they do not have them. That is a very erroneous assumption. It simply is that we have read what Alma said: "It is given unto many to know the mysteries of God; nevertheless they are laid under a strict command that they shall not impart only according to the portion of his word which he doth grant unto the children of men, according to the heed and diligence which they give unto him" (Alma 12:9).

THE SUPERNAL, CONSUMMATE SPIRITUAL GIFT

Now the supernal, consummate spiritual gift! And it is so simple and so present that we often ignore it. It is almost overwhelming when you come to understand that the Holy Ghost, when it is conferred, is as a gift! Now, those outside of the Church can be influenced by the Holy Ghost—can be inspired by it. That must be true, else how could they receive the inspiration to conversion? But following baptism, we have conferred upon us the gift of the Holy Ghost as a presence. I quote from Moses:

And he also said unto him: If thou wilt turn unto me, and hearken unto my voice, and believe, and repent of all thy transgressions, and be baptized, even in water, in the name of mine Only Begotten Son, who is full of grace and truth, which is Jesus Christ, the only name which shall be given under heaven, whereby salvation shall come unto the children of men, ye shall receive the *gift of the Holy Ghost,* asking all things in his name, and whatsoever ye shall ask, it shall be given you (Moses 6:52; emphasis added).

Then again: "Yea, behold, I will tell you in your mind and in your heart, by the Holy Ghost, which shall come upon you and which shall dwell in your heart" (D&C 8:2). This is the supernal gift—the one that each one of us has access to if we will.

Angels speak by the power of the Holy Ghost, Nephi, chiding some of his associates, after talking along these same lines, said:

> Wherefore, now after I have spoken these words, if ye cannot understand them it will be because ye ask not, neither do ye knock; wherefore, ye are not brought into the light, but must perish in the dark.
>
> For behold, again I say unto you that if ye will enter in by the way, and receive the Holy Ghost, it will show unto you all things what ye should do. (2 Nephi 32:4–5.)

TESTIMONY

Now in testimony. Here we are as Latter-day Saints, members of The Church of Jesus Christ of Latter-day Saints. We have the gospel. We are pressed going to and fro with the necessities of life, of living in mortality, and that part of our existence is quite in order. The Lord prayed unto the Father for the Apostles that they were not to be taken out of the world but that they should be kept from sin.

We are not to be of the world. We are to be in the world but not of the world. And in the world we have the right, if we would live for it, to be possessed of quiet spiritual guidance if we will not seek for the manifestations of it, if we will not seek after signs. If we will live to be worthy, there will attend us a guiding spirit that will preclude our doing anything in mortality, if we are obedient, that would ultimately interfere with our exaltation and our right to return to the presence of Him who is our Father.

Now, do not despise the things of the Spirit. Do not set them second after things that are intellectual. Intellectually we want the evidence, we want the proof, *we seek after the signs!* It is that spiritual part of our nature, which we must accept on pure faith, that prepares us to receive the supernal gifts.

And I affirm to you, as one who has the right to that witness, that Jesus is the Christ, the Son of God, the Only Begotten of the Father; that these gifts are present with the Church; that angels have not ceased to appear and administer to men, nor will they so long as time shall last or earth shall stand or there shall be one man upon the face thereof to be saved.

These things have not ceased, for in The Church of Jesus Christ of Latter-day Saints there is that great power of faith, and it dwells in each one of you. As you say your humble prayers, you might humbly appeal to the Lord that the gift of faith might be yours for His purposes, and that these gifts, if He will, might come to you, that you might serve others.

PART FOUR

Agency

14

The Choice

IT USED TO BE A PRACTICE, NO LONGER held, that the Brethren would hold a social following a general conference. On one of these occasions the program centered on the opening of a jubilee box prepared by the Relief Society of the Box Elder Stake in Brigham City fifty years ago to celebrate the centennial of the Church.

The box included newspapers, mementos, and a few letters. One of those letters was written by my grandmother, Sarah Adeline Wight Packer. I quote:

> We moved to a farm in Corinne in the year 1902. There being no branch of the Church there at that time . . . , myself and Hannah Basley visited all the sisters in Corinne and surrounding territory, to see if there was enough interest among them to organize a Relief Society.
>
> Through our visits we learned the sisters were willing to come to meeting, and so we proceeded to get a branch organized.

MESSAGE TO POSTERITY

There was another jubilee box at our social. Each couple posed for a portrait, and we were given a page on which to write a message to go into it. The box will be closed at year's end, to be opened in the year 2030.

Address given at general conference October 1980.

What my wife and I wrote in our message is summarized in these thoughts directed to our children and grandchildren.

The counsel I give is very difficult to teach and to learn. I fear that when I have given this counsel, some will say, "Well, I knew that already," and regard it as prosaic, unimaginative, even dull. For what I want to communicate is so ordinary, so commonplace, that it is very difficult to have it universally regarded as important.

Nevertheless, we want our children and grandchildren to know that, beyond the fundamental truth that Jesus is the Christ, the Son of God, there has been a restoration of His gospel through the prophets, that the fulness of the gospel is upon the earth. After that (really as an essential part of it), this is the one truth we most want to teach our children.

ANCESTORS

Years ago I spent a day with Sister Packer in the record office in London. We were looking for Mary Haley. Like missionaries looking for living souls, we tracted through the pages of old record books. Some of them, I am sure, had not been opened for a hundred years.

I spent most of the day reading the minutes of the overseers of the workhouse—which was really the poorhouse.

One entry told of a woman who had been dismissed from the workhouse and sent to prison. She was refused permission to leave to check on a report that her child was being badly abused at the workhouse school. In great frustration she had "willfully broken a window." And so they sent her to prison.

Another entry reported an inspection of the school. The doctor complained that piles of manure along the edge of the school yard blocked the drainage. Water and sewage had backed up into the yard until the mire was ankle deep. Because of the cold and the poor condition of the children's shoes, many children were ill.

The record of dismissals listed "dead" or "died" time after time, with an explanation: "complaint," "fever," "consumption," "dropsy."

We found Mary Haley! She married Edward Sayers, and they had eleven children. Six of them died before they were seven years of age, one from burns. To our knowledge, only one of the eleven grew to maturity.

That was Eleanor Sayers, my wife's great-grandmother. She was born at Pullham, Norfolk, in the Depwade Union Workhouse and was the first of her family to join the Church. She died of cancer in a dismal London hospital.

The lives of those souls, our forebears, were characterized from beginning to end by both poverty and obscurity.

Before Eleanor Sayers Harman died, she gave all of her funds to her daughter Edith and counseled her to go to America.

Edith had been cast out by her husband when she joined the Church. She and eight-year-old Nellie left England with the flimsy assurance that a missionary *thought* his family in Idaho might take them in until they could be located.

Nellie was my wife's mother; Edith, her grandmother. I knew them well. They were women of special nobility.

Our lineage runs also to the stately manor houses of England, well connected with the courts of kings, where culture and plenty were much in evidence.

But the dignity and worth of those forebears is not more, and may well be less, than that of Eleanor Sayers.

ROYALTY OF RIGHTEOUSNESS

Sarah and Eleanor, Edith and Nellie—all were women of a special nobility, the royalty of righteousness. We want our children to remember that their lineage runs to the poorhouse in Pullham, Norfolk, and to remember this: It is the misapprehension of most people that if you are good, really good, at what you do, you will eventually be both widely known and well compensated.

It is the understanding of almost everyone that success, to be complete, must include a generous portion of both fame and fortune as essential ingredients.

The world seems to work on that premise. The premise is false. It is not true. The Lord taught otherwise.

TRUE HAPPINESS IS NOT BASED ON WEALTH OR FAME

I want you, our children, to know this truth:

You need not be either rich or hold high position to be completely successful and truly happy.

In fact, if these things come to you, and they may, true success must be achieved in spite of them, not because of them.

It is remarkably difficult to teach this truth. If one who is not well known, and not well compensated, claims that he has learned for himself that neither fame nor fortune are essential to success, we tend to reject his statement as self-serving. What else could he say and not count himself a failure?

If someone who has possession of fame or fortune asserts that neither matters to success or happiness, we suspect that his expression is also self-serving, even patronizing.

Therefore, we will not accept as reliable authorities either those who have fame and fortune or those who have not. We question that either can be an objective witness.

That leaves only one course open to us: trial and error—to learn for oneself, by experience, about prominence and wealth or their opposites.

We thereafter struggle through life, perhaps missing both fame and fortune, to finally learn one day that one can, indeed, succeed without possessing either. Or we may, one day, have both and learn that neither has made us happy; neither is basic to the recipe for true success and for complete happiness. That is a very slow way to learn.

Was it Poor Richard who said, "Experience keeps a dear school, but fools will learn in no other"? (*The Autobiography of Benjamin Franklin, Poor Richard's Almanac, and Other Papers* [New York: A. L. Burt Co., n.d.], p. 230.)

We come into mortal life to receive a body and to be tested, to learn to choose.

DECISION BETWEEN GOOD AND EVIL

We want our children and their children to know that the choice of life is not between fame and obscurity, nor is the choice between wealth and poverty. The choice is between good and evil, and that is a very different matter indeed.

When we finally understand this lesson, thereafter our happiness will not be determined by material things. We may be happy without them or successful in spite of them. Wealth and prominence do not always come from having earned them. Our worth is not measured by renown or by what we own.

Someone may say that my testimony may not be valid because of the prominence of the General Authorities of the Church. That is something we do not earn. It comes, as the saying goes, "with the territory." And I want you to know that it comes as a burden on our backs, not as wings on our heels.

Our lives are made up of thousands of everyday choices. Over the years these little choices will be bundled together and show clearly what we value.

The crucial test of life, I emphasize, does not center in the choice between fame and obscurity, nor between wealth and poverty. The greatest decision of life is between good and evil.

We may foolishly bring upon ourselves unhappiness and trouble, even suffering. These are not always to be regarded as penalties imposed by a displeased Creator. They are part of the lessons of life, part of the test.

Some are tested by poor health, some by a body that is deformed or homely. Others are tested by handsome and healthy bodies; some by the passion of youth; others by the erosions of age.

Some suffer disappointment in marriage, family problems; others live in poverty and obscurity. Some (perhaps this is the hardest test) find ease and luxury.

All are part of the test, and there is more equality in this testing than sometimes we suspect.

It is possible to be both rich and famous and at the same time succeed spiritually. But the Lord warned of the difficulty of it when He talked of camels and needles (see Matthew 19:24).

SEEK FIRST THE KINGDOM OF GOD

This message is central to the scriptures. The Book of Mormon tells us that "men are instructed sufficiently that they know good from evil" (2 Nephi 2:5).

We are taught, also, "Men are free according to the flesh; and all things are given them which are expedient unto man. And they are free to choose"—

One: "liberty and eternal life, through the great mediation of all men."

Or, two: "to choose captivity and death, according to the captivity and power of the devil." (2 Nephi 2:27.)

From the Old Testament: "A good name is rather to be chosen than great riches" (Proverbs 22:1).

From the New Testament: "Seek ye first the kingdom of God, and his righteousness; and all these things shall be added unto you" (Matthew 6:33).

Again, from the Book of Mormon:

> Before ye seek for riches, seek ye for the kingdom of God.
> And after ye have obtained a hope in Christ ye shall obtain riches, if ye seek them; and ye will seek them for the intent to do good—to clothe the naked, and to feed the hungry, and to liberate the captive, and administer relief to the sick and the afflicted. (Jacob 2:18–19.)

And from the Doctrine and Covenants:

> Seek not for riches but for wisdom, and behold, the mysteries of God shall be unfolded unto you, and then shall you be made rich (D&C 6:7).

> Behold, he that hath eternal life is rich (D&C 11:7).

FORMULA FOR SUCCESS

What, then, do we want our children and grandchildren to do? Simply this:

Be good!
Study the gospel.
Live it!
Stay active in the Church.
Receive the ordinances.
Keep your covenants.

I do not know at this time whether our posterity is learning. I do know that what I am teaching is true.

One day each of you will know that some things are not divisible. The love of your parents is one of them. Parents do not love one child more than another—nor less. Each receives all of it.

Position and wealth are no more essential to true happiness in mortality than their absence can prevent you from achieving it.

I can envision a day, in the generations ahead, when I would regard you and your children, and theirs, struggling with the challenges of life.

I may see you go the full distance of mortality without becoming either well-known or wealthy. I can see myself falling to my knees to thank a generous God that my prayers have been answered, that you have succeeded, that you are truly happy.

We now move into an uncertain future. But we are not uncertain. Oh, my children, bear testimony, build Zion. Then you will find true success, complete happiness.

15

Our Moral Environment

I HAVE BEEN A GENERAL AUTHORITY and a member of the Quorum of the Twelve Apostles for many years. During this time I have interviewed I don't know how many—surely thousands—of members of the Church and have talked with them in intimate terms of their worthiness, their sorrow, and their happiness. I only mention that in the hope that the credential of experience may persuade you to consider matters which have us deeply worried.

My message is to members of the Church as an environmentalist. It is not on the physical but on the moral and spiritual environment in which we must raise our families. As we test the moral environment, we find the pollution index is spiraling upward.

The Book of Mormon depicts humanity struggling through a "mist of darkness" and defines the darkness as the "temptations of the devil" (1 Nephi 8:23; 12:17). So dense was that moral pollution that many followed "strange roads" and "fell away into forbidden paths and were lost" (see 1 Nephi 8:23–32).

The deliberate pollution of the fountain of life now clouds our moral environment. The gift of mortal life and the capacity to kindle other lives is a supernal blessing. Its worth is incalculable!

THE SPIRITUAL ENVIRONMENT

The rapid, sweeping deterioration of values is characterized by a preoccupation—even an obsession—with the procreative act. Abstinence before marriage and fidelity within it are openly

---

Address given at general conference April 1992.

scoffed at—marriage and parenthood ridiculed as burdensome, unnecessary. Modesty, a virtue of a refined individual or society, is all but gone.

THE TEMPTER

The adversary is jealous toward all who have the power to beget life. He cannot beget life; he is impotent. He and those who followed him were cast out and forfeited the right to a mortal body. His angels even begged to inhabit the bodies of swine (see Matthew 8:31). And the revelations tell us that "he seeketh that all men might be miserable like unto himself" (2 Nephi 2:27).

With ever fewer exceptions, what we see and read and hear have the mating act as a central theme. Censorship is forced off-stage as a violation of individual freedom.

That which should be absolutely private is disrobed and acted out center stage. In the shadows backstage are addiction, pornography, perversion, infidelity, abortion, and—the saddest of them all—incest and molestation. In company with them now is a plague of biblical proportions. And all of them are on the increase.

Society excuses itself from responsibility except for teaching the physical process of reproduction to children in school to prevent pregnancy and disease and providing teenagers with devices which are supposed to protect them from both.

When any effort is made to include values in these courses—basic universal values, not just values of the Church, but of civilization, of society itself—the protest arises, "You are imposing religion upon us, infringing upon our freedom."

FREEDOM TO CHOOSE

While we pass laws to reduce pollution of the earth, any proposal to protect the moral and spiritual environment is shouted down and marched against as infringing upon liberty, agency, freedom, the right to choose.

It is interesting how one virtue, when given exaggerated or fanatical emphasis, can be used to batter down another, with freedom, a virtue, invoked to protect *vice*. Those determined to transgress see any regulation of their lifestyle as interfering with their agency and seek to have their actions condoned by making them legal.

People who are otherwise sensible say, "I do not intend to indulge, but I vote for freedom of choice for those who do."

Regardless of how lofty and moral the "pro-choice" argument sounds, it is badly flawed. With that same logic one could argue that all traffic signs and barriers which keep the careless from danger should be pulled down on the theory that each individual must be free to choose how close to the edge he will go.

The phrase *"free* agency" does not appear in scripture. The only agency spoken of there is *moral agency,* "which," the Lord said, "I have given unto him, that every man may be *accountable* for his own sins in the day of judgment" (D&C 101:78; emphasis added).

And the Lord warned members of His Church, "Let not that which I have appointed be polluted by mine enemies, *by the consent of those who call themselves after my name:* for this is a very sore and grievous sin against me, and against my people" (D&C 101:97–98; emphasis added).

Because the laws of man, by and large, do not raise moral issues, we are taught to honor, sustain, and obey the law (see Articles of Faith 1:12), and that "he that keepeth the laws of God hath no need to break the laws of the land" (D&C 58:21).

When a moral issue does arise, it is the responsibility of the leaders of the Church to speak out. Gambling, for instance, certainly is a moral issue. Life is a moral issue. When morality is involved, we have both the right and the obligation to raise a warning voice. We do not as a church speak on political issues unless morality is involved. In thirty years and thousands of interviews, I have never once asked a member of the Church what political party they belonged to.

PHYSICAL AND MORAL LAWS

There are both moral and physical laws "irrevocably decreed in heaven before the foundations of this world" (D&C 130:20) which man cannot overrule.

For instance, do you think a vote to repeal the law of gravity would do any good?

Suppose a law decreed that all children would be taken from their parents and raised by the state. Such a law would be wicked but probably could be enforced. Such things have been done before.

But suppose an article of that law stated, "Within fifteen days the mother will cease all emotional ties to her child."

That provision would be absolutely unenforceable. No matter how severe the penalty or the number of enforcers, it is absolutely unenforceable because it contravenes both natural and moral law.

No matter if fifteen weeks or months or fifteen years were allowed, it cannot be enforced! It may work with animals, but "all flesh," the scriptures teach, "is not the same flesh: but there is one kind of flesh of men, another flesh of beasts" (1 Corinthians 15:39). It cannot be made to work with human mothers. Never!

A man-made law against nature would be as impossible to defend as a law annulling love between mother and child would be impossible to enforce!

CHILDREN OF GOD

No greater ideal has been revealed than the supernal truth that we are the children of God, and we differ, by virtue of our creation, from all other living things (see Moses 6:8–10, 22, 59).

No idea has been more destructive of happiness, no philosophy has produced more sorrow, more heartbreak and mischief; no idea has done more to destroy the family than the idea that we are not the offspring of God but only advanced animals, compelled to yield to every carnal urge.

Animals are not subject to moral law. Nevertheless, while by and large they are promiscuous in responding to their mating instincts, their mating rituals have set patterns and have rigid limitations. For instance, animals do not pair up with their own gender to satisfy their mating instincts. Nor are these instincts expressed in the molestation of their offspring.

The source of life is now relegated to the level of unwed pleasure, bought and sold and even defiled in satanic rituals. Children of God can willfully surrender to their carnal nature and, without remorse, defy the laws of morality and degrade themselves even below the beasts.

ABOMINABLE SIN

If we pollute our fountains of life, there will be penalties "exquisite" and "hard to bear" (see D&C 19:15), more than all of the physical pleasure ever could be worth. Alma told his son Corianton: "Know ye not, my son, that these things are an abomination in the sight of the Lord; yea, most abominable above all sins save it be the shedding of innocent blood or denying the Holy Ghost?" (Alma 39:5.)

The code for moral law is found in the scriptures, stated as simply as, "Wickedness never was happiness" (Alma 41:10). The scriptures speak in general terms, leaving us free to apply the principles of the gospel to meet the infinite variety of life. But when they say "thou shalt not," we had better pay attention.

The only legitimate employment of the power of procreation is between husband and wife, man and woman, who have been legally and lawfully married. Anything else violates the commandments of God. From Alma, "If ye speak against it, it matters not, for the word of God must be fulfilled" (Alma 5:58).

THE MEASURE OF A SUCCESSFUL PARENT

It is a great challenge to raise a family in the darkening mists of our moral environment.

We emphasize that the greatest work you will do will be within the walls of your home (see Harold B. Lee, *Ensign,* July 1973, p. 98), and that "no other success can compensate for failure in the home" (David O. McKay, *Improvement Era,* June 1964, p. 445).

The measure of our success as parents, however, will not rest solely on how our children turn out. That judgment would be just only if we could raise our families in a perfectly moral environment, and that now is not possible.

It is not uncommon for responsible parents to lose one of their children, for a time, to influences over which they have no control. They agonize over rebellious sons or daughters. They are puzzled over why they are so helpless when they have tried so hard to do what they should.

It is my conviction that those wicked influences one day will be overruled.

The Prophet Joseph Smith declared—and he never taught a more comforting doctrine—that the eternal sealings of faithful parents and the divine promises made to them for valiant service in the Cause of Truth, would save not only themselves, but likewise their posterity. Though some of the sheep may wander, the eye of the Shepherd is upon them, and sooner or later they will feel the tentacles of Divine Providence reaching out after them and drawing them back to the fold. Either in this life or the life to come, they will return. They will have to pay their debt to justice; they will suffer for their sins; and may tread a thorny path; but if it leads them at last, like the penitent Prodigal, to a loving and forgiving father's heart and home, the painful experience will not have been in vain. Pray for your careless and disobedient children; hold on to them with your faith. Hope on, trust on, till you see the salvation of God. (Orson F. Whitney, in Conference Report, April 1929, p. 110.)

We cannot overemphasize the value of temple marriage, the binding ties of the sealing ordinance, and the standards of worthiness required of them. When parents keep the covenants they have made at the altar of the temple, their children will be forever bound to them. President Brigham Young said:

> Let the father and mother, who are members of this Church and kingdom, take a righteous course, and strive with all their might never to do a wrong, but to do good all their lives; if they have one child or one hundred children, if they conduct themselves towards them as they should, binding them to the Lord by their faith and prayers, I care not where those children go, they are bound up to their parents by an everlasting tie, and no power of earth or hell can separate them from their parents in eternity; they will return again to the fountain from whence they sprang (quoted in Joseph Fielding Smith, *Doctrines of Salvation,* comp. Bruce R. McConkie, 3 vols. [Salt Lake City: Bookcraft, 1954–56], 2:90–91).

REPENTANCE

In the battle of life, the adversary takes enormous numbers of prisoners, and many who know of no way to escape and are pressed into his service. Every soul confined to a concentration camp of sin and guilt has a key to the gate. The adversary cannot hold them if they know how to use it. The key is labeled *Repentance.* The twin principles of repentance and forgiveness exceed in strength the awesome power of the adversary.

I know of no sins connected with the moral standard for which we cannot be forgiven. I do not exempt abortion. The formula is stated in forty words: "Behold, he who has repented of his sins, the same is forgiven, and I, the Lord, remember them no more. By this ye may know if a man repenteth of his sins—behold, he will confess them and forsake them." (D&C 58:42–43.)

I WILL REMEMBER YOUR SINS NO MORE

However long and painful the process of repentance, the Lord has said:

This is the covenant . . . I will make with them. . . . I will put my *laws* into their hearts, and in their minds will I write them;

And *their sins and iniquities will I remember no more.* (Hebrews 10:16–17; emphasis added.)

Civilizations, like Sodom and Gomorrah, destroyed themselves by disobedience to the laws of morality. "For the Spirit of the Lord will not always strive with man. And when the Spirit ceaseth to strive with man then cometh speedy destruction." (2 Nephi 26:11; see also Genesis 6:3; Ether 2:15; D&C 1:33; Moses 8:17.)

God grant that we will come to our senses and protect our moral environment from this mist of darkness which deepens day by day. The fate of all humanity hangs precariously in the balance.

And may we have the protection of Him who is our Father and our God, and may we merit the love and blessings of His Son, our Redeemer.

16

Agency and Control

SOME YEARS AGO I HAD IN MY OFFICE a four-star general and his wife. They were very impressive people. They admired the Church because of the conduct of our youth. The general's wife mentioned her children, of whom she was justly proud. But she expressed a deep concern. "Tell me," she said, "how you are able to control your youth and build such character as we have seen in your young men?"

I was interested in her use of the word *control*. The answer, I told them, centered in the doctrines of the gospel. They were interested; so I spoke briefly of the doctrine of agency. I said we develop control by teaching freedom. Perhaps at first they thought we start at the wrong end of the subject. A four-star general is nothing if not a disciplinarian. But when one understands the gospel, it becomes very clear that the best control is self-control.

It may seem unusual at first to foster self-control by centering on freedom of choice, but it is a very sound doctrinal approach.

While either subject may be taught separately, and though they may appear at first to be opposites, they are in fact parts of the same subject.

Some who do not understand the doctrinal part do not readily see the relationship between obedience and agency. And they miss one vital connection and see obedience only as restraint. They then resist the very thing that will give them true freedom. There is no true freedom without responsibility, and there is no enduring freedom without a knowledge of the truth. The Lord said, "If ye

---

Address given at general conference April 1983.

continue in my word, then are ye my disciples indeed; and ye shall know the truth, and the truth shall make you free" (John 8:31–32).

The general quickly understood a truth that is missed even by some in the Church. Latter-day Saints are not obedient because they are compelled to be obedient. They are obedient because they know certain spiritual truths and have decided, as an expression of their own individual agency, to obey the commandments of God.

We are the sons and daughters of God, willing followers, disciples of the Lord Jesus Christ, and "under this head [we] are made free" (Mosiah 5:8).

Those who talk of blind obedience may appear to know many things, but they do not understand the doctrines of the gospel. There is an obedience that comes from a knowledge of the truth that transcends any external form of control. We are not obedient because we are blind, we are obedient because we can see. The best control, I repeat, is self-control.

The general knew then why we teach our children the doctrines of the gospel of Jesus Christ and where they get the resolute determination to protect individual freedom.

Responsibility for teaching the doctrines rests upon parents. "The glory of God is intelligence, or, in other words, light and truth. Light and truth forsake [the] evil one. . . . I have commanded you to bring up *your children* in light and truth." (D&C 93:36, 37, 40; emphasis added.)

If all your children know about the gospel is what you have taught them at home, how safe will they be? Will they reject evil because they choose to reject it?

As a young man in the military service, I visited the ancient shrine at Nikko Kanko in Japan. There, carved into the facade of a building, are the three monkeys. One with its hands over its ears, another with hands over its eyes, and the third with hands over its mouth. Hear no evil; see no evil; speak no evil! That is easier said than done! It is not easy to foster self-control when the world is teaching indulgence.

Fortunately, there is very substantial help for parents. Unfortunately, some families overlook it.

Several years ago I attended a seminary graduation in Hawaii. A handsome young Hawaiian athlete was being honored. He had been blessed with a well-formed body, and he had excelled in several sports. As athletes often are, he was well known both in and out of the Church. His athletic coaches had trained him for the most part in the coordination of his physical powers, adding a little on such virtues as determination and courage.

He said it had not been difficult for him to achieve athletically. If he practiced and kept the training rules, the muscles of his body responded as he wished and he had coordination and control.

Then he talked of a control that did not come easy, and said: "I found it is easier to control the muscles in my arms and legs than to control the muscles in my tongue. I found it easier to control my eyes on the playing field than on the street. It is not easy to control what I will hear. Most of all, it is not easy to control my thoughts." He then expressed gratitude for the seminary program and paid tribute to his seminary teachers. They were the coaches who taught him control over the most permanent part of his nature.

It is not long before the ability to throw a ball or leap a barrier or lift a weight becomes incidental in life. Physical prowess fades. But moral and spiritual strength can grow stronger as the physical part of us weakens with age.

If you want your children to grow spiritually, teach them the doctrines of the gospel.

If you want your son to play the piano, it is good to expose him to music. This may give him a feel for it and help greatly in his learning. But this is not enough. There is the practice and the memorization and the practice and the practice and the practice before he can play it well.

If you want your daughter to learn a language, expose her to those who speak it. She may get a feel for the language, even pick up many words. But this is not enough. She must memorize grammar and vocabulary. She must practice pronunciation. There is rote learning without which she will never speak or write the language fluently.

So it is with the gospel. One may have a feel for it. But at some time one must learn the doctrine. Here, too, rote learning, practice, memorization, reading, listening, discussion—these all become essential. There is no royal road to learning.

The Church can help parents because this kind of learning is effectively given in a classroom setting. So we have seminaries, institutes, religion classes; there are priesthood, Sunday School, and auxiliary classes. The curriculum for all of them centers in the scriptures and the history of the Church. Spiritual development is tied very closely to a knowledge of the scriptures, where the doctrines are found.

A school library may hold a world of knowledge. But unless a student knows the system of cataloging, a search for that knowledge will be discouraging; it will be an ordeal. Those systems are really not too difficult to learn. Then all of the knowledge in all of the books is opened to the student. Searching becomes very simple indeed. But one must find it and read it. One must *earn* it.

It is so with the scriptures. They contain the fulness of the everlasting gospel, an eternity of knowledge. But one must learn to use them or the search will be discouraging. Again, there is a system. Learn about the concordance, the footnotes, the Topical Guide; memorize the books of the Bible and the Book of Mormon. The scriptures will then yield their treasure. All of this is taught in the seminary and institute classes. The teachers are both worthy and well trained. But they cannot help if your students are not enrolled.

There is a revolution in progress. The silicone chip has changed our future. We move from the Industrial Age to the Age of Information. And schools are tooling up to meet the challenge. Graduation requirements for high schools and entrance requirements for colleges are being tightened up. Elective courses are being reduced in number, and they must be carefully selected.

Without guidance, your student may choose another elective

instead of seminary, or another course instead of an institute class. That would surely be a mistake. It would be like adding one more brick to the house of knowledge when there is little mortar to hold it all together. Parents, encourage, even insist, that your students register for seminary or institute. Presidents, bishops, youth leaders, you are responsible to encourage every youngster, without exception, to enroll. Few things you do will benefit them quite as much.

Students, if your values are in place, you will not hesitate to forego an elective class that may decorate your life in favor of instruction which can hold together the very foundation of it. Then, once enrolled, attend, study, and learn. Persuade your friends to do the same. You will never regret it; this I promise you.

Parents, you are greatly indebted to teachers. Somehow you must show it by supporting them. Very few teachers are unworthy of support. If there is a problem, too frequently and all too quickly some parents side with their child against a teacher. As a rule of thumb, my wife and I have told our youngsters that disrespect for teachers, in public schools or in Church schools, brings trouble at home as well. This year two hundred thousand students are enrolled in seminary, and over one hundred and twenty thousand in institutes of religion in eighteen languages in sixty-eight countries. Whether it be released-time, the early-morning, or the home-study programs, the courses are the same. They center in the scriptures; they teach the doctrine and history of the Church.

Some classes are very humble indeed. President Spencer W. Kimball and I once attended a seminary class in North Dakota. We did not meet in a fine room with a blackboard and projector and special school chairs. We met in a very small bedroom in a very small house.

The teacher, Sister Two Dogs, sat on the edge of the bed. The students crowded together on the floor. It was no less a class than one held in a beautiful building. The most important ingredient, the Spirit of the Lord, was there. I attended a seminary graduation in Omaha, Nebraska. The speaker, again a young man, described this experience.

"Each morning I awoke to the sweet voice of my mother calling out, 'John, John, time to get ready for seminary!' The year rolled on and the mornings grew cold and wet and dark; still the happy voice of Mother would sing out, 'John, John, time to get up for seminary!'" Then he added, "I learned to hate that sound!"

But then, choking back the tears, he thanked his mother for what she had given him. And I think only later did he realize that she had to be up first every morning.

The temptation your children will face will not come at home or in the seminary class. It will come later, when they are away from both teacher and parent. One day you must set them free. When that day comes, how free will they be, and how safe? It will depend on how much truth they have received. I know of a young missionary who, half a world away from his parents and teachers, faced the testing that comes to young manhood. There, beyond the control of either of them, he made a decision. Later he wrote: "I'm so glad I stayed, because during this last month I found something—I found myself."

I thank God for teachers in the Church, you who have chosen, and have been chosen for, the better part.

In those discouraging hours before immature, disinterested, and sometimes impudent students, may you hear a voice as well. That still, small voice of inspiration whispering, "Teach ye diligently and my grace shall attend you" (D&C 88:78).

17

The Word of Wisdom: The Principle and the Promises

How grateful we are for you, our youth. *Nothing* is more precious than our children, our youth. It is to the youth of the Church that I give this counsel.

Several years ago in Africa I learned how dangerously invisible crocodiles can be. I then warned our youth about unseen spiritual crocodiles lying in wait to destroy them.

Those invisible dangers have greatly increased in number, and now there are many kinds of them.

Some of them are like land mines hidden about in a field you must cross on your way to maturity. Neighborhoods and schools, which once were safe, are no longer secure. Fortunately you have within you a spiritual power much like a mine detector. If you learn how it works, it will warn you of the presence of unseen crocodiles and mines, and you can avoid trouble.

REGULATIONS OF THE WORD OF WISDOM

Three years after the organization of the Church, a revelation came which described our day in these prophetic words: "Behold, verily, thus saith the Lord unto you: In consequence of evils and designs which do and will exist in the hearts of conspiring men in the last days, I have warned you, and forewarn you, by giving unto you this word of wisdom by revelation" (D&C 89:4).

The Word of Wisdom put restrictions on members of the Church. To this day those regulations apply to every member and

---

Address given at general conference April 1996.

to everyone who seeks to join the Church. They are so compelling that no one is to be baptized into the Church without first agreeing to live by them. No one will be called to teach or to lead without accepting them. When you want to go to the temple, you will be asked if you keep the Word of Wisdom. If you do not, you cannot go to the house of the Lord until you are fully worthy.

We know that young people generally don't like restrictions. Believe it or not, we were young once and we remember.

A resistance to anything that limits one's conduct has almost taken over society. Our whole social order could self-destruct over the obsession with freedom disconnected from responsibility, where choice is imagined to be somehow independent of consequences.

Young people must understand that there is something of colossal importance to justify the restrictions imposed by the Word of Wisdom!

While the revelation came first as a "greeting; not by commandment or constraint" (D&C 89:2), when members of the Church had had time to be taught the import of the revelation, succeeding Presidents of the Church declared it to be a commandment. And it was accepted by the Church as such.

"A Principle with Promise"

The Word of Wisdom was "given for a principle with promise" (D&C 89:3). That word *principle* in the revelation is a very important one. A principle is an enduring truth, a law, a rule you can adopt to guide you in making decisions. Generally principles are not spelled out in detail. That leaves you free to find your way with an enduring truth, a principle, as your anchor.

Members write in asking if this thing or that is against the Word of Wisdom. It's well known that tea, coffee, liquor, and tobacco are against it. It has not been spelled out in more detail. Rather, we teach the principle together with the promised blessings. There are many habit-forming, addictive things that one can drink or chew or inhale or inject and that injure both body and spirit which are not mentioned in the revelation.

Not everything harmful is specifically listed; arsenic, for instance—certainly bad, but not habit-forming! He who must be commanded in all things, the Lord said, "is a slothful and not a wise servant" (D&C 58:26).

In some cultures, native drinks are claimed to be harmless because they are not specifically mentioned in the revelation. Yet they draw members, particularly men, away from their families to parties which certainly offend the principle. Promises made in the revelation will be denied to the careless or the reckless.

STAY ON THE SAFE SIDE

Obedience to counsel will keep you on the safe side of life.

The story is told of a king who was choosing between two drivers for his coach. He ordered each of them to drive his coach down a steep, winding road cut into a high cliff.

The first driver came down slowly, hugging the wall of the cliff. The second driver demonstrated great talent and ability. He raced down the mountain, with the coach so close at times that half the wheel was off the edge of the cliff.

The king was very thoughtful, then wisely chose the first man to drive his coach. It is best to stay on the safe side of things.

USE MODERATION IN MATTERS OF HEALTH

The Word of Wisdom is "adapted to the capacity of the weak and the weakest of all saints" (D&C 89:3). It is buttressed by other scriptures. They teach that the good things of the earth "are made for the benefit and the use of man, . . . yea," the Lord said, "for food and for raiment, for taste and for smell, to strengthen the body and to enliven the soul, . . . to be used, with judgment, not to excess, neither by extortion" (D&C 59:18–20).

Learn to use moderation and common sense in matters of health and nutrition, and particularly in medication. Avoid being extreme or fanatical or becoming a faddist.

For example, the Word of Wisdom counsels us to eat meat sparingly (see D&C 89:12). Lest someone become extreme, we are told in another revelation that "whoso forbiddeth to [eat meat] is not ordained of God" (D&C 49:18; see note at end of this chapter).

Another scripture counsels, "Cease to be idle; cease to be unclean; . . . cease to sleep longer than is needful; retire to thy bed early, that ye may not be weary; arise early, that your bodies and your minds may be invigorated" (D&C 88:124).

THE PROMISE OF HEALTH

Honor the principle of the Word of Wisdom, and you will receive the promised blessings. "All saints," the revelation promises, "who remember to keep and do these sayings, walking in obedience to the commandments," are promised that they "shall receive health in their navel and marrow to their bones" and "shall run and not be weary, and shall walk and not faint" (D&C 89:18, 20).

The Word of Wisdom does not promise you perfect health, but it teaches how to keep the body you were born with in the best condition and your mind alert to delicate spiritual promptings.

I remember a blessing I received when I was serving in the military. It included counsel that's good for every young person: "You have been given a body of such physical proportions and fitness as to enable your spirit to function through it. . . . You should cherish this as a great heritage. Guard [it] and protect it. Take nothing into it that shall harm the organs thereof because it is sacred. It is the instrument of your mind and [the] foundation of your character." That counsel had great influence on me.

The promise of health for living the standard of the revelation is not limited to members of the Church.

The Promise of Revelation

And then there is a greater blessing promised in the Word of Wisdom. Those who obey it are promised that they "shall find wisdom and great treasures of knowledge, even hidden treasures" (D&C 89:19). This is the personal revelation through which you can detect invisible crocodiles or hidden mines or other dangers.

When you were confirmed a member of the Church, you had conferred upon you the gift of the Holy Ghost. "Know ye not," Paul wrote, "that your body is the temple of the Holy Ghost which is in you?" (1 Corinthians 6:19.)

And the Lord said, "The Comforter, which is the Holy Ghost, whom the Father will send in my name, he shall teach you all things, and bring all things to your remembrance, whatsoever I have said unto you" (John 14:26).

The Promise of Redemption

There's a final promise in the revelation. Speaking again of those who keep and do and obey these commandments, the Lord said, "I . . . give unto them a promise, that the destroying angel shall pass by them, as the children of Israel, and not slay them" (D&C 89:21). That is a remarkable promise.

To understand it, we must turn to the time of Moses. The Israelites had been enslaved for four hundred years. Moses came as their deliverer. He called forth plagues upon Egypt. The Pharaoh agreed each time to free the Israelites, but each time he reneged on his promise. Finally "the Lord said unto Moses, Yet will I bring one plague more upon Pharaoh, and upon Egypt; afterwards he will let you go. . . . All the firstborn in the land of Egypt shall die." (Exodus 11:1, 5.) Moses told the Israelites to "take . . . a lamb . . . without blemish, a male of the first year. . . . Neither shall ye break a bone thereof." (Exodus 12:3, 5, 46; see also John 19:33.)

They were to prepare the lamb as a feast and "take of the blood, and strike it on the . . . door post of the houses. . . . For I will pass through the land of Egypt this night, and will smite all the firstborn in the land . . . : and when I see the blood, I will pass over you, and the plague shall not be upon you to destroy you. . . . And this day . . . ye shall keep . . . by an ordinance for ever." (Exodus 12:7, 12–14.) "When your children shall say unto you, What mean ye by this service? . . . ye shall say, It is the sacrifice of the Lord's passover." (Exodus 12:26–27.)

Surely you see the prophetic symbolism in the Passover. Christ was "the Lamb of God" (John 1:29, 36), the Firstborn, male, without blemish. He was slain without breaking His bones, even though the soldiers were sent to do it.

But it is not from mortal death that we shall be spared in such a passover if we walk in obedience to these commandments, for each of us in time shall die. But there is spiritual death which you need not suffer. If you are obedient, that spiritual death will pass over you, for "Christ our passover is sacrificed for us," the revelation teaches (1 Corinthians 5:7).

While the Word of Wisdom requires strict obedience, in return it promises health, great treasures of knowledge, and that redemption bought for us by the Lamb of God, who was slain that we might be redeemed.

The law of sacrifice was fulfilled with the Crucifixion. The Lord instituted the sacrament in its place. That is the ordinance we shall keep forever! Young people, attend your meetings and partake of the sacrament.

Surely the Word of Wisdom was given so that you may keep the delicate, sensitive, spiritual part of your nature on proper alert. Learn to "listen" to your feelings. You will be guided and warned and taught and blessed.

Go Forward with Faith

Even though young life is always filled with uncertainties, do not fear the future!

Your young dreams can be realized. All of your worthy, natural physical and emotional desires can be satisfied. You can find a companion to whom you can offer a body free from addiction, from depressants, from stimulants, and a mind sensitive to spiritual guidance and impressions.

You can be sealed together for time and for all eternity in a marriage covenant and can express that love freely, which has as its consummate purpose the begetting of life, of children, of family, of happiness.

If you are one who's been wandering off course, now is the time to return. You can, you know. Young people, go forward with faith. You'll be led by the Spirit as was Nephi, "not knowing beforehand the things which [he] should do" (1 Nephi 4:6).

Keep the Word of Wisdom. Seek worthy companions. Attend church faithfully. Never fail daily to seek for help through prayer. And I promise you that the way will be easier and you shall have a composure of mind and a confident attitude toward life and the future. You shall be warned of dangers and shall be guided through the whisperings of the Holy Spirit.

I bear witness that this revelation is a powerful protection to all members of the Church, particularly to the youth of the Church, as you face a life full of so many troubles and danger and uncertainties. But, young members of the Church, have faith. The Lord will be with you; you will be guided.

Note

The context for verse 18 is verse 19: "For, behold, the beasts of the field and the fowls of the air [are] ordained for the use of man for food." Section 49 was specifically directed to members of the United Society of Believers in Christ's Second Appearing (the Shakers) to correct some of their erroneous doctrines. One of their beliefs was not to eat flesh-meat or fish.

PART FIVE

Holiness

18

The Holy Temple

THERE ARE MANY REASONS WHY ONE should want to come to the temple. Even its external appearance seems to hint of its deeply spiritual purposes. This is much more evident within its walls. Over the door to the temple appears the tribute "Holiness to the Lord." When you enter any dedicated temple, you are in the house of the Lord.

In the temples, members of the Church who make themselves eligible can participate in the most exalted of the redeeming ordinances that have been revealed to mankind. There, in a sacred ceremony, an individual may be washed and anointed and instructed and endowed and sealed. And when we have received these blessings for ourselves, we may officiate for those who have died without having had the same opportunity. In the temples sacred ordinances are performed for the living and for the dead alike.

THESE THINGS ARE SACRED

A careful reading of the scriptures reveals that the Lord did not tell all things to all people. There were some qualifications set that were prerequisite to receiving sacred information. Temple ceremonies fall within this category.

We do not discuss the temple ordinances outside the temples. It was never intended that knowledge of these temple ceremonies would be limited to a select few who would be obliged to ensure

---

Ensign article February 1995.

that others never learn of them. It is quite the opposite, in fact. With great effort we urge every soul to qualify and prepare for the temple experience. Those who have been to the temple have been taught an ideal: Someday every living soul and every soul who has ever lived shall have the opportunity to hear the gospel and to accept or reject what the temple offers. If this opportunity is rejected, the rejection must be on the part of the individual himself.

The ordinances and ceremonies of the temple are simple. They are beautiful. They are sacred. They are kept confidential lest they be given to those who are unprepared. Curiosity is not a preparation. Deep interest itself is not a preparation. Preparation for the ordinances includes preliminary steps: faith, repentance, baptism, confirmation, worthiness, a maturity and dignity worthy of one who comes invited as a guest into the house of the Lord.

All who are worthy and qualify in every way may enter the temple, there to be introduced to the sacred rites and ordinances.

WORTHY TO ENTER

Once you have some feeling for the value of temple blessings and for the sacredness of the ordinances performed in the temple, you would be hesitant to question the high standards set by the Lord for entrance into the holy temple.

You must possess a current recommend to be admitted to the temple. This recommend must be signed by the proper officers of the Church. Only those who are worthy should go to the temple. Your local bishop or branch president has the responsibility of making inquiries into your personal worthiness. This interview is of great importance, for it is an occasion to explore with an ordained servant of the Lord the pattern of your life. If anything is amiss in your life, the bishop will be able to help you resolve it. Through this procedure, as you counsel with the common judge in Israel, you can declare or can be helped to establish your worthiness to enter the temple with the Lord's approval.

The interview for a temple recommend is conducted privately between the bishop and the Church member concerned. Here the member is asked searching questions about his personal conduct and worthiness and about his loyalty to the Church and its officers. The person must certify that he is morally clean and is keeping the Word of Wisdom, paying a full tithe, living in harmony with the teachings of the Church, and not maintaining any affiliation or sympathy with apostate groups. The bishop is instructed that confidentiality in handling these matters with each interviewee is of the utmost importance.

Acceptable answers to the bishop's questions will ordinarily establish the worthiness of an individual to receive a temple recommend. If an applicant is not keeping the commandments or there is something unsettled about his life that needs putting in order, it will be necessary for him to demonstrate true repentance before a temple recommend is issued.

After the bishop has conducted such an interview, a member of the stake presidency likewise interviews each of us before we go to the temple.

TAUGHT FROM ON HIGH

Before going to the temple for the first time, or even after many times, it may help you to realize that the teaching in the temples is done in symbolic fashion. The Lord, the Master Teacher, gave much of His instruction in this way.

The temple is a great school. It is a house of learning. In the temples the atmosphere is maintained so that it is ideal for instruction on matters that are deeply spiritual. The late Elder John A. Widtsoe of the Quorum of the Twelve was a distinguished university president and a world renowned scholar. He had great reverence for temple work and said on one occasion:

> The temple ordinances encompass the whole plan of salvation, as taught from time to time by the leaders of the Church, and elucidate matters difficult of understanding. There is no warping or twisting in fitting the temple teachings into the great scheme of salvation. The philosophical completeness of the

endowment is one of the great arguments for the veracity of the temple ordinances. Moreover, this completeness of survey and expounding of the Gospel plan, makes temple worship one of the most effective methods in refreshing the memory concerning the whole structure of the Gospel. (*Utah Genealogical and Historical Magazine,* April 1921, p. 58.)

If you will go to the temple and remember that the teaching is symbolic, you will never go in the proper spirit without coming away with your vision extended, feeling a little more exalted, with your knowledge increased as to things that are spiritual. The teaching plan is superb. It is inspired. The Lord Himself, the Master Teacher, taught His disciples constantly in parables—a verbal way to represent symbolically things that might otherwise be difficult to understand.

The temple itself becomes a symbol. If you have seen one of the temples at night, fully lighted, you know what an impressive sight that can be. The house of the Lord, bathed in light, standing out in the darkness, becomes symbolic of the power and the inspiration of the gospel of Jesus Christ standing as a beacon in a world that sinks ever further into spiritual darkness.

Upon entering the temple you exchange your street clothing for the white clothing of the temple. This change of clothing takes place in the locker room, where each individual is provided with a locker and dressing space that is completely private. In the temple the ideal of modesty is carefully maintained. As you put your clothing in the locker you leave your cares and concerns and distractions there with them. You step out of this private little dressing area dressed in white and you feel a oneness and a sense of equality, for all around you are similarly dressed.

THE POWER TO SEAL

For those of you who look forward to a temple marriage, you may want to know what will occur. We do not quote the words of the sealing (marriage) ordinance outside of the temple, but we may describe the sealing room as being beautiful in its appoint-ment, quiet and serene in spirit, and hallowed by the sacred work that is performed there.

Before the couple comes to the altar for the sealing ordinance it is the privilege of the officiator to extend, and of the young couple to receive, some counsel. These are among the thoughts that a young couple might hear on this occasion.

"Today is your wedding day. You are caught up in the emotion of your marriage. Temples were built as a sanctuary for such ordi-nances as this. We are not in the world. The things of the world do not apply here and should have no influence upon what we do here. We have come out of the world into the temple of the Lord. This becomes the most important day of your lives.

"You were born, invited to earth, by parents who prepared a mortal tabernacle for your spirit to inhabit. Each of you has been baptized. Baptism, a sacred ordinance, is symbolic of a cleansing, symbolic of death and resurrection, symbolic of coming forward in a newness of life. It contemplates repentance and a remission of sins. The sacrament of the Lord's Supper is a renewal of the covenant of baptism, and we can, if we live for it, retain a remis-sion of our sins.

"You, the groom, were ordained to the priesthood. You had first conferred upon you the Aaronic Priesthood and probably have progressed through all the offices thereof—deacon, teacher, and priest. Then the day came when you were found worthy to re-ceive the Melchizedek Priesthood. That priesthood, the higher priesthood, is defined as the priesthood after the holiest order of God, or the Holy Priesthood after the Order of the Son of God (see Alma 13:18; Helaman 8:18; D&C 107:2–4). You were given an office in the priesthood. You are now an elder.

"Each of you has received your endowment. In that endowment you received an investment of eternal potential. But all of these things, in one sense, were preliminary and preparatory to your coming to the altar to be sealed as husband and wife for time and for all eternity. You now become a family, free to act in the creation of life, to have the opportunity through devotion and sacrifice to bring children into the world and to raise them and foster them safely through their mortal existence; to see them come one day, as you have come, to participate in these sacred temple ordinances.

"You come willingly and have been judged to be worthy. To accept one another in the marriage covenant is a great responsibility, one that carries with it blessings without measure."

If we would understand both the history and the doctrine of temple work, we must understand what the sealing power is. We must envision, at least to a degree, why the *keys* of authority to employ the sealing power are crucial—crucial not just to the ordinance work of the temples but to all ordinance work in all the Church throughout the world.

The sealing power represents the transcendent delegation of spiritual authority from God to man. The keeper of that sealing power is the Lord's chief representative here upon the earth, the President of the Church. That is the position of consummate trust and authority.

As has been said, much of the teaching relating to the deeper spiritual things in the Church, particularly in the temple, is symbolic. We use the word *keys* in a symbolic way. Here the keys of priesthood authority represent the limits of the power extended from beyond the veil to mortal man to act in the name of God upon the earth. The words *seal* and *keys* and *priesthood* are closely linked together.

The keys of the sealing power are synonymous with the keys of the everlasting priesthood.

> When Jesus came into the coasts of Caesarea Philippi, he asked his disciples, saying, Whom do men say that I the Son of man am? . . .
>
> And Simon Peter answered and said, Thou art the Christ, the Son of the living God.
>
> And Jesus answered and said unto him, Blessed art thou, Simon Bar-jona: for flesh and blood hath not revealed it unto thee, but my Father which is in heaven.

And I say also unto thee, That thou art Peter, and upon this rock I will build my church; and the gates of hell shall not prevail against it.

And I will give unto thee the keys of the kingdom of heaven: and whatsoever thou shalt bind on earth shall be bound in heaven: and whatsoever thou shalt loose on earth shall be loosed in heaven. (Matthew 16:13–19.)

Peter was to hold the keys. Peter was to hold the sealing power, that authority which carried the power to bind or seal on earth or to loose on earth and it would be so in the heavens. Those keys belong to the President of the Church—to the prophet, seer, and revelator. That sacred sealing power is with the Church now. Nothing is regarded with more sacred contemplation by those who know the significance of this authority. Nothing is more closely held. There are relatively few men who have been delegated this sealing power upon the earth at any given time—in each temple are brethren who have been given the sealing power. No one can get it except from the prophet, seer, and revelator and President of The Church of Jesus Christ of Latter-day Saints.

A clear statement follows regarding the sealing power as binding on all that we do for the living and the dead.

Whenever the fulness of the gospel is on earth, the Lord has agents to whom he gives power to bind on earth and seal eternally in the heavens (Matthew 16:19; 18:18; Helaman 10:3–10; D&C 132:46–49). . . .

All things that are not sealed by this power have an end when men are dead. Unless a baptism has this enduring seal, it will not admit a person to the celestial kingdom; unless an eternal marriage covenant is sealed by this authority, it will not take the participating parties to an exaltation in the highest heaven within the celestial world.

All things gain enduring force and validity because of the sealing power. So comprehensive is this power that it embraces ordinances performed for the living and the dead, seals the children on earth up to their fathers who went before, and forms the enduring patriarchal chain that will exist eternally among exalted beings. (Bruce R. McConkie, *Mormon Doctrine*, 2d ed. [Salt Lake City: Bookcraft, 1966], p. 683.)

In the Church we hold sufficient authority to perform all of the ordinances necessary to redeem and to exalt the whole human family. And, because we have the keys to the sealing power, what we bind in proper order here will be bound in heaven. Those keys—the keys to seal and bind on earth, and have it bound in heaven—represent the consummate gift from our God. With that authority we can baptize and bless, we can endow and seal, and the Lord will honor our commitments.

The Prophet Joseph Smith said he was frequently asked the question, "'Can we not be saved without going through with all those ordinances, etc.?' I would answer, No, not the fullness of salvation. Jesus said, 'There are many mansions in my Father's house, and I will go and prepare a place for you.' House here named should have been translated kingdom; and any person who is exalted to the highest mansion has to abide a celestial law, and the whole law too." (*History of the Church,* 6:184.)

NOT WITHOUT OPPOSITION

Temples are the very center of the spiritual strength of the Church. We should expect that the adversary will try to interfere with us as a church and with us individually as we seek to participate in this sacred and inspired work. Temple work brings so much resistance because it is the source of so much spiritual power to the Latter-day Saints and to the entire Church.

At the Logan Temple cornerstone dedication, President George Q. Cannon made this statement:

Every foundation stone that is laid for a Temple, and every Temple completed according to the order the Lord has revealed for his holy Priesthood, lessens the power of Satan on the earth, and increases the power of God and Godliness, moves the heavens in mighty power in our behalf, invokes and calls down upon us the blessings of the Eternal Gods, and those who reside in their presence (*Millennial Star,* 12 November 1877, p. 743).

When members of the Church are troubled or when crucial decisions weigh heavily upon their minds, it is a common thing for them to go to the temple. It is a good place to take our cares. In the temple we can receive spiritual perspective. There, during the time of the temple service, we are "out of the world."

Sometimes our minds are so beset with problems, and there are so many things clamoring for attention at once, that we just cannot think clearly and see clearly. At the temple the dust of distraction seems to settle out, the fog and the haze seem to lift, and we can "see" things that we were not able to see before and find a way through our troubles that we had not previously known.

The Lord will bless us as we attend to the sacred ordinance work of the temples. Blessings there will not be limited to our temple service. We will be blessed in all of our affairs.

COME TO THE TEMPLE

No work is more of a protection to this Church than temple work and the genealogical research that supports it. No work is more spiritually refining. No work we do gives us more power. No work requires a higher standard of righteousness.

Our labors in the temple cover us with a shield and a protection, both individually and as a people.

So come to the temple—come and claim your blessings. It is a sacred work.

19

Washed Clean

My message is to our young people. We have great concern for young people who grow up without values on which to base their conduct.

Study of Doctrines Improves Behavior

I have long believed that the study of the doctrines of the gospel will improve behavior quicker than talking about behavior will improve behavior.

The study of behavior is greatly improved when linked to standards and to values. Practical values, useful in everyday life, are found in the scriptures and the doctrines they reveal. I will give you one example: "We believe that through the Atonement of Christ, all mankind may be saved, by obedience to the laws and ordinances of the Gospel" (Articles of Faith 1:3).

You should learn while you are young that while the atonement of Christ applies to humanity in general, the influence of it is individual, very personal, and very useful. Even to you beginners, an understanding of the Atonement is of immediate and very practical value in everyday life.

Untidy Service Men in World War II

More than fifty years ago during World War II, I had an experience. Our bomber crew had been trained at Langley Field,

---

Address given at general conference April 1997.

Virginia, to use the latest invention—radar. We were ordered to the West Coast and then on to the Pacific.

We were transported on a freight train with boxcars fitted with narrow bedsprings that could be pulled down from the wall at night. There were no dining cars. Instead, camp kitchens were set up in boxcars with dirt floors.

We were dressed in light-colored summer uniforms. The baggage car got sidetracked, so we had no change of clothing during the six-day trip. It was very hot crossing Texas and Arizona. Smoke and cinders from the engine made it very uncomfortable. There was no way to bathe or wash our uniforms. We rolled into Los Angeles one morning—a grubby-looking outfit—and were told to return to the train that evening.

We thought first of food. The ten of us in our crew pooled our money and headed for the best restaurant we could find.

It was crowded, and so we joined a long line waiting to be seated. I was first, just behind some well-dressed women. Even without turning around, the stately woman in front of me soon became aware that we were there.

She turned and looked at us. Then she turned and looked me over from head to toe. There I stood in that sweaty, dirty, sooty, wrinkled uniform. She said in a tone of disgust, "My, what untidy men!" All eyes turned to us.

No doubt she wished we were not there; I shared her wish. I felt as dirty as I was, uncomfortable, and ashamed.

THE SHAME OF BEING SPIRITUALLY UNCLEAN

Later, when I began a serious study of the scriptures, I noticed references to being spiritually clean. One verse says, "Ye would be more miserable to dwell with a holy and just God, under a consciousness of your filthiness before him, than ye would to dwell with the damned souls in hell" (Mormon 9:4).

I could understand that. I remembered how I felt that day in Los Angeles. I reasoned that to be spiritually unclean would bring shame and humiliation immeasurably more intense than I felt then. I found references—there are at least eight of them—which say that no unclean thing can enter the presence of God (see 1 Nephi 10:21; 15:34; Alma 7:21; 11:37; 40:26; 3 Nephi 27:19; D&C 94:9; Moses 6:57). While I realized those references had little to do with dirty clothes or soiled hands, I decided I wanted to stay spiritually clean.

Incidentally, that day we went canoeing in Griffith Park. We were horsing around and, of course, tipped over. We got to shore all right, and in due time the sun dried us out. By the time we returned to the train, we were really quite presentable.

I learned that when I didn't live as I ought to, getting myself spiritually clean was not as easy as taking a shower or putting on clean clothing or falling out of a canoe.

Repentance Can Cleanse Us

I learned about the great plan of happiness, that we are on earth to be tested. We will all make mistakes. The Apostle John taught, "If we say that we have no sin, we deceive ourselves, and the truth is not in us." Fortunately he added, "If we confess our sins, he is faithful and just to forgive us our sins, and to cleanse us from all unrighteousness." (1 John 1:8–9.) I paid particular attention to that word *cleanse.*

I thought that repentance, like soap, should be used frequently. I found that when I apologized for mistakes, things were better. But for serious mistakes, an apology was not enough—sometimes not even possible. While these mistakes were, for the most part, not major ones, the spiritual pain called *guilt* invariably set in. Sooner or later they must be resolved, but I didn't know what to do. That happens when you break something that you alone can't fix.

"Wickedness Never Was Happiness"

Among you young people are those who are "vexed," as Peter said, "with the filthy conversation of the wicked" (2 Peter 2:7).

Some of you joke about standards and see no need to change behavior. You tell yourselves it doesn't matter because everybody's doing it.

But that doesn't work, because you, by nature, are good. How many times have you heard someone say, after doing some generous or heroic deed or simply helping others, how *good* it made them feel? Like any natural feeling or emotion, that reaction is inborn in you. Surely you have experienced that yourself! Happiness is inseparably connected with decent, clean behavior.

The prophet Alma bluntly told his wayward son that because he transgressed he was "in a state contrary to the nature of happiness" (Alma 41:11) and that "wickedness never was happiness" (v. 10). Those who don't know how to erase mistakes often feel cornered and rebellious and lose themselves in unworthy living. If you travel with transgressors, you will suffer much more than I did in that restaurant.

THROUGH THE ATONEMENT WE CAN REPENT

Most mistakes you can repair yourself, alone, through prayerful repentance. The more serious ones require help. Without help, you are like one who can't or doesn't wash or bathe or put on clean clothes. The path you need to follow is in the scriptures. Read them and your faith in Christ will grow. Listen to those who know the gospel.

You will learn about the fall of man, about the purpose of life, about good and evil, about temptations and repentance, about how the Spirit works. Read what Alma said of his repentance: "I could remember my pains no more; yea, I was harrowed up by the memory of my sins no more" (Alma 36:19).

Hear the Lord say, "Behold, he who has repented of his sins, the same is forgiven, and I, the Lord, remember them no more" (D&C 58:42; see also Hebrews 8:12; 10:17). Doctrine can change behavior quicker than talking about behavior will.

It was through reading the scriptures, and listening, that I could understand, at least in part, the power of the Atonement.

Can you imagine how I felt when finally I could see that if I followed whatever conditions the Redeemer had set, I need never endure the agony of being spiritually unclean? Imagine the consoling, liberating, exalting feeling that will come to you when you see the reality of the Atonement and the practical everyday value of it to you individually.

You need not know everything before the power of the Atonement will work for you. Have faith in Christ; it begins to work the day you ask! The scripture speaks of "obedience to the laws and ordinances of the Gospel" (Articles of Faith 1:3). We all pretty well know what it means to obey laws. But how are we to obey ordinances?

Generally we understand that, conditioned upon repentance, the ordinance of baptism washes our sins away. Some wonder if they were baptized too soon. If only they could be baptized now and have a clean start. But that is not necessary! Through the ordinance of the sacrament, you renew the covenants made at baptism. When you meet all of the conditions of repentance, however difficult, you may be forgiven and your transgressions will trouble your mind no more.

Like Joseph F. Smith, we can be clean. President Joseph F. Smith was six years old when his father, Hyrum, was killed in Carthage Jail. Joseph crossed the plains with his widowed mother. At age fifteen he was called on a mission to Hawaii. He felt lost and alone and said: "I was very much oppressed. . . . I was almost naked and entirely friendless, except the friendship of a poor, benighted . . . people. I felt as if I was so debased in my condition of poverty, lack of intelligence and knowledge, just a boy, that I hardly dared look [anyone] in the face."

While pondering his plight, the young elder had a dream, "a literal thing; . . . a reality." He dreamed he was on a journey rushing as fast as he possibly could.

He carried a small bundle. Finally he came to a wonderful mansion, his destination. As he approached, he saw a notice, "Bath." He turned aside quickly, went in, and washed himself clean. He opened his little bundle and found clean, white cloth-ing—"a thing," he said, "I had not seen for a long time." He put them on and rushed to the door of the mansion.

"I knocked," he said, "and the door opened, and the man who stood there was the Prophet Joseph Smith. He looked at me a little reprovingly, and the first words he said [were]: 'Joseph, you are late.' . . . I took confidence and said:

"'Yes, but I am clean—I am clean!'" (Joseph F. Smith, *Gospel Doctrine,* 5th ed. [1939], pp. 541–42.)

And so it can be with you.

POETIC EXPRESSION OF TESTIMONY

I say to you again that a knowledge of the principles and doc-trines of the gospel will affect your behavior more than talking about behavior.

I have used the Atonement as one of many examples. In the gospel of Jesus Christ are values on which to build a happy life.

I give you my testimony that our Father in Heaven lives. The atonement of Christ can bless your life. If only I could tell you what the Atonement means to me! I once tried to express it in writing, and I close with these lines:

> In ancient times the cry "Unclean!"
> Would warn of lepers near.
> "Unclean! Unclean!" the words rang out;
> Then all drew back in fear,
>
> Lest by the touch of lepers' hands
> They, too, would lepers be.
> There was no cure in ancient times,
> Just hopeless agony.
>
> No soap, no balm, no medicine
> Could stay disease or pain.
> There was no salve, no cleansing bath,
> To make them well again.

But there was One, the record shows,
Whose touch could make them pure;
Could ease their awful suffering,
Their rotting flesh restore.

His coming long had been foretold.
Signs would precede His birth.
A Son of God to woman born,
With power to cleanse the earth.

The day He made ten lepers whole,
The day He made them clean,
Well symbolized His ministry
And what His life would mean.

However great that miracle,
This was not why He came.
He came to rescue every soul
From death, from sin, from shame.

For greater miracles, He said,
His servants yet would do,
To rescue every living soul,
Not just heal up the few.

Though we're redeemed from mortal death,
We still can't enter in
Unless we're clean, cleansed every whit,
From every mortal sin.

What must be done to make us clean
We cannot do alone.
The law, to be a law, requires
A pure one must atone.

He taught that justice will be stayed
Till mercy's claim be heard
If we repent and are baptized
And live by every word. . . .

If we could only understand
All we have heard and seen,
We'd know there is no greater gift
Than those two words—"Washed clean!"
(Boyd K. Packer, "Washed Clean.")

20

The Brilliant Morning of Forgiveness

IN APRIL OF 1847, BRIGHAM YOUNG led the first company of pioneers out of Winter Quarters. At that same time, 1,600 miles to the west, the pathetic survivors of the Donner Party straggled down the slopes of the Sierra Nevada Mountains into the Sacramento Valley.

They had spent the ferocious winter trapped in the snowdrifts below the summit. That any survived the days and weeks and months of starvation and indescribable suffering is almost beyond belief.

Among them was fifteen-year-old John Breen. On the night of April 24 he walked into Johnson's Ranch. Years later John wrote:

> It was long after dark when we got to Johnson's Ranch, so the first time I saw it was early in the morning. The weather was fine, the ground was covered with green grass, the birds were singing from the tops of the trees, and the journey was over. I could scarcely believe that I was alive.
>
> The scene that I saw that morning seems to be photographed on my mind. Most of the incidents are gone from memory, but I can always see the camp near Johnson's Ranch. (John Breen, "Pioneer Memoirs," unpublished, as quoted on "The Americanization of Utah," PBS television broadcast.)

At first I was very puzzled by his statement that "most of the incidents are gone from memory." How could long months of in-

---

Address given at general conference October 1995.

credible suffering and sorrow ever be gone from his mind? How could that brutal dark winter be replaced with one brilliant morning?

On further reflection I decided it was not puzzling at all. I have seen something similar happen to people I have known.

I have seen some who have spent a long winter of guilt and spiritual starvation emerge into the morning of forgiveness. When morning came, they learned this:

"Behold, he who has repented of his sins, the same is forgiven, and I, the Lord, remember them no more" (D&C 58:42).

"I, even I, am he that blotteth out thy transgressions for mine own sake, and will not remember thy sins" (Isaiah 43:25).

"I will forgive their iniquity, and I will remember their sin no more" (Jeremiah 31:34).

"For I will be merciful to their unrighteousness, and their sins and their iniquities will I remember no more" (Hebrews 8:12; see also 10:17).

ALMA FELT THE JOY OF FORGIVENESS

When the prophet Alma was young, he spent such a time "*racked*," as he said, "*with eternal torment, [his] soul . . . harrowed up to the greatest degree*" (Alma 36:12; emphasis added).

He even thought, "Oh, . . . that I could be banished and become extinct both soul and body" (v. 15).

But his mind caught hold of a thought. When he nurtured the thought and acted upon it, the morning of forgiveness came.

> I could remember my pains no more; yea, I was harrowed up by the memory of my sins no more.
>
> And oh, what joy, and what marvelous light I did behold; yea, my soul was filled with joy as exceeding as was my pain! (Vv. 19–20.)

THE PROMISE OF COMPLETE FORGIVENESS

Letters come from those who have made tragic mistakes. They ask, "Can I *ever* be forgiven?"

The answer is yes!

The gospel teaches us that relief from torment and guilt can be earned through repentance. Save for those few who defect to perdition after having known a fulness or who shed innocent blood, there is no habit, no addiction, no rebellion, no transgression, no offense exempted from the promise of complete forgiveness. (See Alma 39:5.)

"Come now, and let us reason together, saith the Lord: though your sins be as scarlet, they shall be as white as snow; though they be red like crimson, they shall be as wool." That is, Isaiah continued, "if ye be willing and obedient." (Isaiah 1:18–19.)

Even that grace of God promised in the scriptures comes only "after all we can do" (2 Nephi 25:23).

You may tell yourself that your transgressions are not spiritually illegal. That will not work; neither will rebellion, nor anger, nor joking about them. You cannot do that. And you don't have to do it.

REPENTANCE: THE WAY BACK

There is a way back. It will not help if, out of tender regard for your feelings, I avoid telling you about the hard part.

John Breen did not come to that morning at Johnson's Ranch simply by desiring it. He wallowed and clawed his way up over the pass, suffering every step of the way. But once he knew he would survive and the suffering would end, surely he did not complain at the ordeal. And he had help all the way down. He was with rescuers.

When an offense is minor, as simple a thing as an apology will satisfy the law. Most mistakes can be settled between the individual and the Lord, and that should be done speedily (see D&C

109:21). It requires a confession to Him, and whatever obvious repairs need to be made.

With sincere repentance as a pattern in our lives, measured by our willingness to "confess them and forsake them" (D&C 58:43; see also Ezekiel 18:21–24, 31–32), the Lord has promised that we may "always *retain* a remission of [our] sins" (Mosiah 4:12; emphasis added).

Alma bluntly told his wayward son that "repentance could not come unto men except there were a punishment" (Alma 42:16).

The punishment may, for the most part, consist of the torment we inflict upon ourselves. It may be the loss of privilege or progress. (Forgiveness will come eventually to all repentant souls who have not committed the unpardonable sin [see Matthew 12:31].) Forgiveness does not, however, necessarily ensure exaltation (see D&C 132:38–39; see also Psalm 16:10; Acts 2:25–27; Joseph Smith, *Teachings of the Prophet Joseph Smith,* sel. Joseph Fielding Smith [Salt Lake City: Deseret Book Co., 1938], pp. 339, 356, 357). We are punished *by* our sins, if not *for* them.

There are some transgressions that require a discipline which will bring about the relief that comes with the morning of forgiveness. If your mistakes have been grievous ones, go to your bishop. Like the rescuers who brought John Breen down from the mountaintops, bishops can guide you through the steps required to obtain forgiveness insofar as the Church is concerned. Each one of us must work out individually forgiveness from the Lord.

THE NEED TO MAKE RESTITUTION

To earn forgiveness, one must make restitution. That means you give back what you have taken or ease the pain of those you have injured.

But sometimes you *cannot* give back what you have taken because you don't have it to give. If you have caused others to suffer unbearably—defiled someone's virtue, for example—it is not within your power to give it back.

There are times you cannot mend that which you have broken. Perhaps the offense was long ago, or the injured refused your penance. Perhaps the damage was so severe that you cannot fix it no matter how desperately you want to.

Your repentance cannot be accepted unless there is a restitution. If you cannot undo what you have done, you are trapped. It is easy to understand how helpless and hopeless you then feel and why you might want to give up, just as Alma did.

The thought that rescued Alma, when he acted upon it, is this: Restoring what you cannot restore, healing the wound you cannot heal, fixing that which you broke and you cannot fix is the very purpose of the atonement of Christ.

When your desire is firm and you are willing to pay the "uttermost farthing" (Matthew 5:25–26), the law of restitution is suspended. Your obligation is transferred to the Lord. He will settle your accounts.

Comforting Knowledge

I repeat, save for the exception of the very few who defect to perdition or who shed innocent blood, there is no habit, no addiction, no rebellion, no transgression, no apostasy, no crime exempted from the promise of complete forgiveness. That is the promise of the atonement of Christ.

How all can be repaired, we do not know. It may not all be accomplished in this life. We know from visions and visitations that the servants of the Lord continue the work of redemption beyond the veil (see D&C 138).

This knowledge should be as comforting to the innocent as it is to the guilty. I am thinking of parents who suffer unbearably for the mistakes of their wayward children and are losing hope.

We Cannot Condone Unworthy Conduct

Some members wonder why their priesthood leaders will not accept them just as they are and simply comfort them in what they call pure Christian love.

Pure Christian love, the love of Christ, does not presuppose approval of all conduct. Surely the ordinary experiences of parenthood teach that one can be consumed with love for another and yet be unable to approve unworthy conduct.

We cannot, as a church, approve unworthy conduct or accept into full fellowship individuals who live or who teach standards that are grossly in violation of that which the Lord requires of Latter-day Saints.

If we, out of sympathy, should approve unworthy conduct, it might give present comfort to someone but would not ultimately contribute to that person's happiness (see *Teachings of the Prophet Joseph Smith*, pp. 256–57).

In the most tender of sermons in the revelations on kindness and long-suffering, on meekness, gentleness, on love unfeigned, the Lord instructs us to reprove "betimes with sharpness, when moved upon by the Holy Ghost; and then [show] forth afterwards an increase of love toward him whom thou hast reproved" (D&C 121:43).

SEEK RELIEF NOW

The Lord provides ways for us to pay our debts to Him. In one sense we ourselves may participate in an atonement. When we are willing to restore to others that which we have not taken, or heal wounds that we did not inflict, or pay a debt that we did not incur, we are emulating His part in the Atonement.

So many live with accusing guilt when relief is ever at hand. So many are like the immigrant woman who skimped and saved and deprived herself until, by selling all of her possessions, she bought a steerage-class ticket to America.

She rationed out the meager provisions she was able to bring with her. Even so, they were gone early in the voyage. When others went for their meals, she stayed below deck—determined to suffer through it. Finally, on the last day, she must, she thought, afford one meal to give her strength for the journey yet ahead. When she asked what the meal would cost, she was told that all of the meals had been included in the price of her ticket.

Never Give Up Hope

That great morning of forgiveness may not come at once. Do not give up if at first you fail. Often the most difficult part of repentance is to forgive yourself. Discouragement is part of that test. Do not give up. That brilliant morning will come.

Then "the peace of God, which passeth . . . understanding" comes into your life once again (Philippians 4:7). Then you, like Him, will remember your sins no more. How will you know? You will know! (See Mosiah 4:1–3.)

Some years ago I was in Washington, D.C., with President Harold B. Lee. Early one morning he called me to come into his hotel room. He was sitting in his robe reading *Gospel Doctrine,* by President Joseph F. Smith, and he said, "Listen to this!

"'Jesus had not finished his work when his body was slain, neither did he finish it after his resurrection from the dead; although he had accomplished the purpose for which he then came to the earth, he had not fulfilled all his work. And when will he? Not until he has redeemed and saved every son and daughter of our father Adam that have been or ever will be born upon this earth to the end of time, except the sons of perdition. That is his mission. We will not finish our work until we have saved ourselves, and then not until we shall have saved all depending upon us; for we are to become saviors upon Mount Zion, as well as Christ. We are called to this mission.'" (Joseph F. Smith, *Gospel Doctrine,* 5th ed. [Salt Lake City: Deseret Book Co., 1939], p. 442.)

"There is never a time," the Prophet Joseph Smith taught, "when the spirit is too old to approach God. All are within the reach of pardoning mercy, who have not committed the unpardonable sin." (*Teachings of the Prophet Joseph Smith,* p. 191.)

And so we pray, and we fast, and we plead, and we implore. We love those who wander, and we never give up hope.

I bear witness of Christ and of the power of His atonement. And I know that "his anger kindleth against the wicked; they repent, and in a moment it is turned away, and they are in his favor, and he giveth them life; therefore, weeping may endure for a night, but joy cometh in the morning" (JST, Psalm 30:5; see also D&C 61:20).

21

A Temple to Exalt

SAY THE WORD *TEMPLE*. SAY IT QUIETLY and reverently. Say it over and over again. *Temple. Temple. Temple.* Add the word *holy*. *Holy Temple.* And you say it as though it were capitalized, no matter where it appears in the sentence.

Temple. One other word is equal in importance to a Latter-day Saint. *Home.* Put the words *holy temple* and *home* together, and you have described what a temple is. The house of the Lord!

The Saints had been commanded to build the first temple at Kirtland. There they had received revelations and knew what the word *temple* meant. There were to have been temples at Independence, at Far West, and on Spring Hill at Adam-ondi-Ahman, but those temples were never started.

The Saints built a temple at Nauvoo but it was destroyed by the mobs.[1] Colonel Thomas L. Kane wrote: "They succeeded in parrying the last sword-thrust" of the mobs until "as a closing work, they placed, on the entablature of the front . . .

The House of the Lord:
Built by The Church of Jesus Christ of Latter-day Saints.
Holiness to the Lord!

". . . It was this day," he wrote, that "saw the departure of the last elders, and the largest band that moved in one company together. The people of Iowa have told that from morning to night they passed westward like an endless procession. They did not seem greatly out of heart, they said; but, at the top of every hill

---

Ensign article August 1993.

before they disappeared, were to be seen looking back, like banished Moors, on their abandoned homes, and the far-seen Temple and its glittering spire."[2]

They left their farms and homes and the temple to their persecutors and disappeared beyond the western horizon, beyond Far West, where the cornerstones, set seven years earlier, were still in place. It was into oblivion, as their persecutors thought. Not quite! They had prophets and Apostles who had the keys of the priesthood, who carried in their minds the ordinances of the house of the Lord, and they knew of the covenants. And, they had the authority to administer them.

It would be thirty years before those ordinances would be written down and forty-seven years until the Salt Lake Temple was completed. But this they knew to be a work of the eternities; that the ordinances revealed to them were "instituted from before the foundation of the world."[3] They knew as well that therein were "the keys of the holy priesthood ordained."[4]

When the Saints trickled into the Salt Lake Valley, a pathetic band of refugees, all they owned was carried in a wagon box or in a handcart. All they could hope to get must come the same way or they must make it themselves.

Nevertheless, on 28 July 1847 Brigham Young announced: "Here we will build a temple to our God."[5] He was a prophet, a seer—and he had *seen* in vision a temple and sketched it out.[6]

It is one thing to see it standing today, walled in to keep out the confusion of a bustling city. It is quite another to picture the pioneers pacing through the sagebrush marking off the temple site before even the rudest log home was built. That they imagined to do it at all is almost beyond belief.

There was an architect in the first company of pioneers, William Weeks, who had designed the Nauvoo Temple. But the stark life of the pioneer, the hopeless desolation and the Moses-like leadership of Brigham Young were too much for him. When President Young was back in Winter Quarters in 1848, Brother Weeks left the Valley, saying, "They will never build the temple without me."[7]

Brigham Young said: "We can build our temple without his assistance, altho' he says we cannot."[8] Truman O. Angell, a carpenter, was appointed to replace Brother Weeks. "If the President and my brethren feel to sustain a poor worm of the dust like me to be Architect of the Church," he said, "let me . . . serve them and not disgrace myself. . . . May the Lord help me to do so."[9]

The isolation which gave them some relief from the mobs was itself an obstacle. Where would they get heavy sledgehammers and wedges with which to split out building blocks of granite? They didn't carry many of those in handcarts or in wagon boxes, either. Where would they get a chisel to carve the moldings or glass to fill the windows?

A great principle was demonstrated to the Church in connection with the choice of building materials. In the October conference of 1852 it was unanimously decided that "we build [the] temple of the best materials [available] in the mountains of North America." It was well known that "President Young was in favor of adobe and pebbles, and it was regarded by many as settled that this view would be adopted."[10] But there is the principle of presidency and the system of councils in the organization the Lord revealed to the Saints. President Young had counselors, and there was the Twelve. After lengthy counseling on the matter, strong-willed President Young yielded and the temple was built of granite.

He was not the only one who had seen the temple in vision. President Wilford Woodruff said: "Before we came to the Rocky Mountains, I had a dream. I dreamed of being in these mountains, and of seeing a large fine looking temple erected in one of these valleys which was built of cut granite stone. . . . Whenever President Young held a council of the brethren of the Twelve and talked of building the temple of adobe or brick, . . . I would say to myself, 'No, you will never do it;' because I had seen it in my dream built of some other material."[11]

It was on the twenty-third anniversary of the organization of the Church, 6 April 1853, that the cornerstone was put in place and the construction officially began.

It would be years before the railroad would cross the Rocky Mountains from the East and the Sierras from the West to meet at a point north of the Great Salt Lake. For years ox teams had been dragging granite stones from the mountains twenty miles to the southeast.

" 'Good morning, Brother,' one man was heard to say to a teamster. 'We missed you at the meetings yesterday afternoon.' 'Yes,' said the driver of the oxen, 'I did not attend meeting. I did not have clothes fit to go to meeting.' 'Well,' said the speaker, 'Brother Brigham called for some more men and teams to haul granite blocks for the Temple.'

"The driver, his whip thrown over his oxen, said, 'Whoa, Haw, Buck, we shall go and get another granite stone from the quarry.' "[12]

At the quarry President Woodruff had watched men cut out granite stones seventy feet square and split them up into building blocks.[13] If there was no mishap, and that would be an exception, the teamster, "too poorly clad to worship," could return within a week.[14]

In due time the railroad came south and a spur was run to the quarry and to Temple Square. Then the stones could reach Temple Square in one day. The canal being dug to convey the granite stones to Temple Square would thereafter be used to carry irrigation water.

On Temple Square the stones were shaped into blocks for the walls, for oval windows and treads; for the four circular staircases which rise up through the corner towers, six hundred eighty-eight steps, all of them exactly alike—each of them weighing over 1,700 pounds, each taking weeks to chisel out and polish.

Symbols are chiseled on the granite stones which depict the sun, the stars, the planets, and the earth. To be sure that the stones representing the phases of the moon were accurate, Elder Orson Pratt, a competent astronomer, set up an observatory on temple block. He could open the slats in the roof to study the heavens with a three-inch lens.

The symbolism is not mysterious. The clouds with rays of

sunlight shining through are immortalized in Elder Parley P. Pratt's great anthem: "The morning breaks, the shadows flee; Lo Zion's standard is unfurled! The dawning of a brighter day . . . majestic rises on the world."[15]

The Big Dipper, with the pointers ranging to the North Star, means that the lost may find their way by the aid of the priest-hood.

The east towers represent the Melchizedek Priesthood and the west towers the Aaronic Priesthood.

These and all the other symbols were carefully drafted by the architect, Truman O. Angel, under the watchful eye of President Brigham Young.[16]

That wicked spirit which had inspired Governor Boggs of Missouri to issue the extermination order against the Saints in 1838 broods forever over the work of the Lord. President Brigham Young had predicted: "We never begin to build a temple without the bells of hell beginning to ring." He added: "I want to hear them ring again. All the tribes of hell will be on the move, if we uncover the walls of this temple."[17] President Young had said when they entered the Valley: "If the people of the United States will let us alone ten years we would ask no odds of them."[18] Ten years to the day after they entered the valley the pioneers were celebrating the 24th of July in the canyons when a messenger arrived with word that Johnston's army was marching west to settle the "Mormon question." Colonel Thomas Kane came to mediate.

President Young told him: "[We] have been driven from place to place; . . . we have been scattered and peeled. . . . We have transgressed no law, . . . neither do we intend to; but as for any nation's coming to destroy this people, God Almighty being my helper, they cannot come here."[19]

It was Colonel Kane who worked out the agreement under which the army was permitted to enter the valley and move through the city to a place beyond.

The First Presidency ordered the settlements evacuated and the Saints to move south. Every evidence of construction was cleared away from Temple Square. All the stones were hidden.

The foundation, which, after seven years' work, was now nearing ground level, was covered over and the block was plowed. It looked then like a field ready to plant.

After peace was established and work could resume, the dirt was removed from the foundation of the temple, which at places was thirty-two feet deep. They found a crack or two running from the foundation stones down to the large rubble stones which formed the footings. A decision must be made! President Young refused to make it without revealed instruction. After seeking counsel from those around him and through that spirit of revelation which was constant with him, he ordered the foundations torn out and replaced.

Since human nature has not changed, one can imagine that there were murmurings. "If he is a prophet, why could not he have gotten that revelation a year ago, or five years ago? Now all that work is wasted." Not so! President Young said: "When the Temple is built I want it to stand though the millennium, in connection with many others that will yet be built."[20] Someone asked Brigham Young once if they would ever live to see the temple completed. He responded: "I do not know. . . . This I do know: There should be a temple built here."[21]

They counted on the principle of the arch on each window distributing the immense weight of the stone above it. When the foundation was replaced with shaped granite stones, sixteen large inverted arches were built into it. There is no record as to why they decided to do that. That manner of construction was then unknown in this country.

If someday perchance there be a massive force wanting to lift the temple from beneath, the arches may well act to distribute the pressure.

The work proceeded with various interruptions. It becomes more of a miracle when one considers what else was done during that period of time. While the building of the Salt Lake Temple might have, during the forty years of its construction, consumed all of the time and energy and resources of the Church, the work was moving forward. Three temples were dedicated during that period of time; 364 communities were founded by the Church in the United States, Canada, and Mexico; the translation of the standard works in the languages proceeded; missions were opened in many parts of the world.

Construction inched upward slowly but surely. A family coming to April conference might notice little difference from the previous April, for only one or two courses of stone might have been placed in the meantime. And a young couple showing their little children about the construction site, as they explained what a temple is and why it must be built with care, might return to the yet unfinished building to teach the same lesson to teenaged grandchildren.

It is not to be wondered that Satan, the enemy of all righteousness, should want to disrupt, to delay, and to destroy both the construction of temples and the work that goes on within them. Opposition rose again, and Congress voted to disenfranchise the Church. In March of 1887, the Edmunds-Tucker Act became effective. Church properties, including the Salt Lake Temple, were escheated to the government. The unfinished temple stood firmly on a foundation of stone; the work of construction went forward on a foundation of faith. For eight years the Church would pay rent on the temple block. It was not until Utah became a state in 1896 that the properties and some of the rent money were returned to the Church.

In 1892 the capstone was laid, and it was unanimously determined to dedicate the temple one year later.

The problem of providing heat and light had been solved years earlier when the temple was at ground level. Natural gas was discovered in Farmington Bay. It was piped to the temple block and they began to drill channels through the granite walls to conduct gas into all the rooms.

Then, about three years before the dedication, electricity became available. They converted the new gas chandeliers, which had been lovingly made by the quorums of elders, and the electric wires were run through the conduits already drilled up through the granite walls.

When the structure was closed in, attention was turned to the interior, which was to exceed in beauty the exterior. In 1890 John Fairbanks, John Hafen, Lorus Pratt, and Edwin Evans were set apart as missionaries to France. They were to learn to paint and sculpt, for the temple would be beautiful within, "so that the Lord's name may be glorified and his cause advanced through . . . the arts."[22]

Brother Fairbanks left seven children for his wife to look after. He could not bear to part with her in public, so two of the children walked with him to the station for a tearful parting.[23] Each wife encouraged her husband to go. The women contributed no less than the men to the building of the temple. Perhaps only another woman can know the sacrifice a woman makes to see that something that must be done, that she cannot do herself, is done. And only a good man knows in his heart of hearts the depth of his dependency upon his wife; how she alone makes worth doing that which must be done, even at great personal sacrifice. The artists were called back when the rooms were ready, and they came with sketches and plans that pleased the Brethren.

A year later, James F. Woods was set apart as a missionary to England to gather genealogies in anticipation of the completion of the temple.[24] How could Brother Woods know that he was pioneering a family history work beyond anything that had been imagined in the mind of man.

Eventually the day of dedication came. In the immense crowd was a seven-year-old boy from Tooele who would carry a clear memory of that event and of President Wilford W. Woodruff for another ninety years. LeGrand Richards would one day serve in the Quorum of Twelve Apostles as his father before him had done.

When he was twelve, LeGrand heard President Woodruff give his last public address. Even after ninety years, Elder Richards bore clear testimony to us of those sacred events.

There have been many visitations to the temple that are of significance to individuals or to the Church. President Lorenzo Snow saw the Savior there. Most of these sacred experiences remain unrecorded or unpublished. Solemn assemblies have been held.

Through the years the day-to-day work of administering ordinances to the living and the dead has proceeded at an ever-increasing pace.

And so the temple was finished. It had been seventy years since the angel Moroni appeared to Joseph Smith and quoted the words with which Malachi the prophet had closed the Old Testament:

> Behold, I will reveal unto you the Priesthood, by the hand of Elijah the prophet, before the coming of the great and dreadful day of the Lord.
>
> And he shall plant in the hearts of the children the promises made to the fathers, and the hearts of the children shall turn to their fathers.
>
> If it were not so, the whole earth would be utterly wasted at his coming.[25]

It had been fifty-seven years since the Lord appeared in the newly completed temple at Kirtland and with him Elijah the prophet, thus fulfilling the prophecy spoken by Malachi more than twenty-two hundred years earlier.

It had been fifty-two years since the Lord commanded the Saints to build a temple in Nauvoo. "For there is not a place found on earth that he may come to and restore again that which was lost unto you, or which he hath taken away, *even the fulness of the priesthood.*"[26]

He gave them a stern warning that they were to complete it within the allotted time:

> But I command you, all ye my saints, to build a house unto me; and I grant unto you a sufficient time to build a house unto me; and during this time your baptisms shall be acceptable unto me.
>
> But behold, at the end of this appointment your baptisms for your dead shall not be acceptable unto me; and if you do not these things at the end of the appointment ye shall be rejected as a church, with your dead, saith the Lord your God.

For verily I say unto you, that after you have had sufficient time to build a house to me, wherein the ordinance of baptizing for the dead belongeth, and for which the same was instituted from before the foundation of the world, your baptisms for your dead cannot be acceptable unto me;

For therein are the *keys of the holy priesthood* ordained, that you may receive honor and glory.[27]

It had been fifty-one years since Joseph Smith, in an epistle to the Saints, revealed the will of the Lord concerning the redemption of both the living and the dead and said:

Brethren, shall we not go on in so great a cause? Go forward and not backward. Courage, brethren, and on, on to the victory! Let your hearts rejoice, and be exceedingly glad. Let the earth break forth into singing. Let the dead speak forth anthems of eternal praise to the King Immanuel, who hath ordained, before the world was, that which would enable us to redeem them out of their prison; for the prisoners shall go free.

Let the mountains shout for joy, and all ye valleys cry aloud.[28]

"The Spirit of God" was sung for the first time at the dedication of the temple at Kirtland, and the building was engulfed in celestial fire. It was sung at the dedication of the Salt Lake Temple. Added was the "Hosanna Anthem": "The house of the Lord is completed, the house of the Lord is completed! May our offering to him be accepted."[29] As the voices of the Saints rose in singing "The Spirit of God like a fire is burning,"[30] surely the mountains did shout for joy and the valleys did cry aloud.

As the Salt Lake Temple was dedicated and given to the Lord as His house, the Hosanna Shout echoed in the everlasting hills. The work was finished, and at once the greater work was just begun. It had been forty years since ground had been broken. Thousands of Saints had foregone the comforts and conveniences of life, had given up even the necessities; and more than a few had literally worn out their lives in the building of the temple. Three other temples had been dedicated, the gospel had been taken across the world, a civilization had been built in the mountains, and now the words of Isaiah the prophet were fulfilled:

> And it shall come to pass in the last days, that the mountain of the Lord's house shall be established in the top of the mountains, and shall be exalted above the hills; and all nations shall flow unto it.
>
> And many people shall go and say, Come ye, and let us go up to the mountain of the Lord, to the house of God of Jacob; and he will teach us of his ways, and we will walk in his paths: for out of Zion shall go forth the law, and the word of the Lord from Jerusalem.[31]

It was not the granite nor the mortar nor the carved work nor the indescribably beautiful appointments that mattered most. Other temples would be built. As we celebrated the centenary, there were forty-five temples across the world. None are less important. However more imposing the temple at Salt Lake City may be, that invisible temple that lives in the building itself is the same in all temples. The ordinances are the same, the covenants equally binding, the blessings equally in force, the Holy Spirit of Promise equally present.

And the center of it all is another temple.

> Know ye not that ye are the temple of God, and that the Spirit of God dwelleth in you?
>
> If any man defile the temple of God, him shall God destroy; for the temple of God is holy, which temple ye are.[32]

> Know ye not that your body is the temple of the Holy Ghost which is in you, which ye have of God, and ye are not your own?
>
> For ye are bought with a price: therefore glorify God in your body, and in your spirit, which are God's.[33]

On the day that the cornerstones were laid for the Salt Lake Temple, President Brigham Young said, "Very few of the Elders of Israel, now on earth, . . . know the meaning of the word endowment. To know, they must experience; and to experience, a temple must be built."[34] Surely it could be said today that very few of those who have experienced the endowment fully appreciate or fully know the supernal worth of the temple ordinances and the family history work which sustains them. This work is crucial to the redemption of both the living and the dead. It is this doctrine more than any other we teach which sets The Church of Jesus Christ of Latter-day Saints apart from all of Christianity and must justify the Restoration.

In preparation for the dedication of the Salt Lake Temple, the First Presidency issued an epistle to the Saints. It is timeless. If it had been written today, it would apply as well as it did one hundred years ago.

> To the Officers and Members of the Church of Jesus Christ of Latter-day Saints:
>
> The near approach of the date for the dedication of the Temple of our God moves us to express with some degree of fullness our feelings to our brethren, the officers of the Church, who with us bear the Priesthood of the Son of God, and to the Latter-day Saints generally; to the end that in entering that holy building we may all be found acceptable ourselves, with our households, and that the building which we shall dedicate may also be acceptable unto the Lord.
>
> The Latter-day Saints have used their means freely to erect other temples in these valleys, and our Father has blessed us in our efforts. Today we enjoy the great happiness of having three of these sacred structures completed, dedicated to and accepted of the Lord, wherein the Saints can enter and attend to those ordinances which He, in His infinite goodness and kindness, has revealed. But for forty years the hopes, desires, and anticipations of the entire Church have been centered upon the completion of

this edifice in the principal city of Zion. Its foundation was laid in the early days of our settlement in these mountains; and from that day until the present, the eyes of the members of the Church in every land have been lovingly directed toward it. Looking upon it as the Temple of temples, the people during all these years have labored with unceasing toil, undiminished patience, and ungrudging expenditure of means to bring it to its present condition of completion; and now that the toils and the sacrifices of forty years are crowned so successfully and happily; now that the great building is at last finished and ready to be used for divine purposes, need we say that we draw near an event whose consummation is to us as a people momentous in the highest degree? Far-reaching in its consequences, as that occasion is certain to be, what remains for us to say in order to impress the entire Church with a sense of its tremendous importance?

On this point, surely nothing; yet may we offer a few words upon a phase that directly touches it. No member of the Church who would be deemed worthy to enter that sacred house can be considered ignorant of the principles of the Gospel. It is not too much to presume that every one knows what his duty is to God and to his fellowman. None is so forgetful as to have lost sight of the admonition that we must be filled with love for and charity toward our brethren. And hence none can for a moment doubt the supreme importance of every member of the congregation being at peace with all his or her brethren and sisters, and at peace with God. How else can we hope to gain the blessings He has promised save by complying with the requirements for which those blessings are the reward!

Can men and women who are violating a law of God, or those who are derelict in yielding obedience to His commands, expect that the mere going into His holy house and taking part in its dedication will render them worthy to receive, and cause them to receive, His blessing?

Do they think that repentance and turning away from sin may be so lightly dispensed with?

Do they dare, even in thought, thus to accuse our Father of injustice and partiality, and attribute to Him carelessness in the fulfillment of His own words?

Assuredly no one claiming to belong to His people would be guilty of such a thing.

Then must those who are unworthy cease to expect a blessing from their attendance at the Temple while sin unrepented of still casts its odor about them, and while bitterness or even an unforgiving coolness exists in their hearts against their brethren and sisters.

On this latter subject we feel that much might be said. In the striving after compliance with the apparently weightier matters of the law, there is a possibility that the importance of this spirit of love and kindness and charity may be underestimated. For ourselves, we cannot think of any precept that at present requires more earnest inculcation.

During the past eighteen months there has been a division of the Latter-day Saints upon national party lines. Political campaigns have been conducted, elections have been held, and feelings, more or less intense, have been engendered in the minds of brethren and sisters upon one side and the other.

We have been cognizant of conduct and have heard of many expressions that have been very painful to us and have grieved our spirits.

We know they have been an offense unto the God of peace and love, and a stumbling block unto many of the Saints.

We feel now that a time for reconciliation has come; that before entering into the Temple to present ourselves before the Lord in solemn assembly, we shall divest ourselves of every harsh and unkind feeling against each other; that not only our bickerings shall cease, but that the cause of them shall be removed, and every sentiment that prompted and has maintained them shall be dispelled; that we shall confess our sins one to another, and ask forgiveness one of another; that we shall plead with the Lord for the spirit of repentance, and, having obtained it, follow its promptings; so that in humbling ourselves before Him and seeking forgiveness from each other, we shall yield that charity and generosity to those who crave our forgiveness that we ask for and expect from heaven.

Thus may we come up into the holy place with our hearts free from guile and our souls prepared for the edification that is promised! Thus shall our supplications, undisturbed by a thought of discord, unitedly mount into the ears of Jehovah and draw down the choice blessings of the God of Heaven!

As your brethren, sustained by your vote and in your faith as the First Presidency of the Church, we have this to say to the Latter-day Saints, in our individual as well as our official capacity: If there is a single member of the Church who has feelings against us, we do not wish to cross the threshold of the Temple until we have satisfied him and have removed from him all cause of feelings, either by explanation or by making proper amends and atonement; neither would we wish to enter the sacred portals of that edifice until we have sought an explanation, or amends, or atonement, from any against whom we may have either a real or fancied grievance.

In now announcing this course for ourselves, we say to all the other officers of the Church that we desire them to follow our example. We wish them from the highest to the lowest and throughout all the Stakes and Wards of Zion to take heed of this counsel. Let them invite all who may have feelings against them to come forward and make them known; let them then endeavor to correct any misapprehensions or misunderstandings which may exist, or give redress for any wrong or injury that may have been done.

We say the same—and when the officers have taken the course indicated we wish them to say the same—to the individual members of the Church. We call upon them to seek to have the fellowship of their brethren and their sisters, and their entire confidence and love; above all to seek to have the fellowship and union of the Holy Ghost. Let this spirit be sought and cherished as diligently within the smallest and humblest family circle, as within the membership of the highest organization and quorum. Let it permeate the hearts of the brothers and sisters, the parents and children of the household, as well as the hearts of the First Presidency and Twelve. Let it mellow and soften all differences between members of the Stake Presidencies and the High Councils, as well as between neighbors living in the same ward. Let it unite young and old, male and female, flock and shepherd, people and Priesthood, in the bonds of gratitude and forgiveness and love, so that Israel may feel approval of the Lord, and that we may all come before Him with a conscience void of offense before all men. Then there will be no disappointment as to the blessings promised those who sincerely worship Him. The sweet whisperings of the Holy Spirit will be given to them and the treasures of heaven, the communion of angels, will be added from time to time, for His promise has gone forth and it cannot fail!

Asking God's blessing upon you all in your endeavor to carry out this counsel, and desirous of seeing it take the form of a united effort on the part of the whole people, we suggest that Saturday, March 25th, 1893, be set apart as a day of fasting and prayer. On that occasion we advise that the Presidencies of Stakes, the High Councils, the Bishops and their Counselors, meet together with the Saints in their several meeting houses, confess their sins one to another, and draw out from the people all feelings of anger, of distrust, or of unfriendliness that may have found a lodgment; so that entire confidence may then and there be restored and love from this time prevail through all the congregations of the Saints.

Wilford Woodruff,

George Q. Cannon,

Joseph F. Smith,

First Presidency of the Church of Jesus Christ of Latter-day Saints, 18 March 1893.[35]

The Lord had promised the Saints at Nauvoo:

If ye labor with all your might, I will consecrate that spot [the temple site] that it shall be made holy.

And if my people will hearken unto my voice, and unto the voice of my servants whom I have appointed to lead my people, behold, verily I say unto you, they shall not be moved out of their place.

But if they will not hearken to my voice, nor unto the voice of these men whom I have appointed, they shall not be blest.[36]

Surely then if we hearken to His voice, and the voice of His servants, we will not be moved from the place the Lord has prepared for each of us.

NOTES

1. Don F. Colvin, "A Historical Study of the Mormon Temple at Nauvoo, Illinois," (thesis, Brigham Young University, Aug. 1962).

2. Pamphlet, discourse delivered before The Historical Society of Pennsylvania, 26 Mar. 1850, Archives Division, Church Historical Department, The Church of Jesus Christ of Latter-day Saints, Salt Lake City, Utah; hereafter cited as Church Archives.

3. D&C 124:33.

4. D&C 124:34.

5. Journal History of The Church of Jesus Christ of Latter-day Saints, 28 July 1847, Church Archives.

6. *Contributor,* vol. 14, no. 6 (Apr. 1893): 260.

7. See Thomas Bullock Journal, 8 July 1848, Church Archives.

8. Ibid.

9. Truman O. Angell Journal, 1857 to 8 Apr. 1868, 28 May 1867, Church Archives.

10. *Contributor,* vol. 14, no. 6 (Apr. 1893): 249.

11. *Journal of Discourses,* 21:299–300.

12. David O. McKay, Salt Lake Temple dedication services, 21 May 1963, pp. 7–8.

13. Journal of Wilford Woodruff, 4 July 1890, Church Archives.

14. David O. McKay, Salt Lake Temple dedication services, 21 May 1963, pp. 7–8.

15. *Hymns,* 1985, no. 1.

16. Truman O. Angell, "The Salt Lake City Temple," *Millennial Star,* vol. 36, no. 18 (5 May 1874): 274–75.

17. *Discourses of Brigham Young,* comp. John A. Widtsoe (Salt Lake City: Deseret Book Co., 1977), p. 410.

18. *Journal of Discourses,* 5:226.

19. *Journal of Discourses,* 5:226.

20. *Journal of Discourses,* 11:372.

21. *Contributor,* vol. 14, no. 6 (Apr. 1893): 257.

22. John Fairbanks Diary, Harold B. Lee Library, Brigham Young University, Provo, Utah.

23. Ibid.

24. Abraham H. Cannon Journal, 13 July 1891, Harold B. Lee Library, Brigham Young University, Provo, Utah.

25. D&C 2:1–3.

26. D&C 124:28; emphasis added.

27. D&C 124:31–34; emphasis added.

28. D&C 128:22–25.

29. "Hosanna Anthem," in Evan Stephens, *The Choir Book,* p. 69.

30. *Hymns,* 1985, no. 2.

31. Isaiah 2:2–3.

32. 1 Corinthians 3:16–17.

33. 1 Corinthians 6:19–20.

34. *Discourses of Brigham Young,* pp. 415–16.

35. *Contributor,* vol. 14, no. 6 (Apr. 1893): 284–85.

36. D&C 124:42–46.

Index

— A —

Aaronic Priesthood, 147, 172
Abortion, 4, 6, 24, 121, 126
Abstinence, 120
Abuse, 6, 24, 26, 31
Accountability, 25–26
Activities, out-of-home, 7, 20
Adam-ondi-Ahman, Mo., 168
Addiction, 24, 31, 121, 135–36,
    139–40, 162, 164
Adversary. *See* Satan
Agency, 43, 85, 87, 117–19,
    121–22, 128–33, 135
Alma, on forgiveness, 161
    on gifts of the spirit, 97–98
    on moral laws, 124
    on mysteries, 108
    on repentance, 155, 163, 164
    on simple things, 65
    was wayward, 85, 155
    "Wickedness never was happi-
    ness," 124, 155
Amalekites, 19
Amulek, 85
Andrew (Apostle), 42
Angell, Truman O., 170, 172
Angels, 90, 102, 106
    speak by power of Holy Ghost,
    48, 85, 109
Animal instincts, 27
Animals, 122–23

Apartments, 68
Apathy, 107
Apology, 154, 162
Apostasy, 8, 45–46, 54, 164
Apostate groups, 145
Apostle, meaning of term, 47
Apostles, are chosen by Jesus
    Christ, 45
    are prophets, seers, and revela-
    tors, 17, 46–47
    are united with First Presidency,
    50–51
    bridge the line of authority,
    16–17, 21
    bring unity of the faith, 18–19
    and conferences, 41–42
    critics of, 49–50
    have the gift of discernment,
    48–49
    heed the counsel of the, 51
    Jesus prayed for, 109
    as living witnesses, 18
    ministry of the, 47–48
    receive revelation, 5
    and the Restoration, 45–46
    as special witnesses, 51–52
    statue of ancient, 18
    sustaining of the, 15
    and temples, 169
Artists, 175
Atheism, 4
Athlete (story), 57

Atonement. *See* Jesus Christ
Authority, of General Authorities,
	43–44
	line of, 16, 21

— B —

Baptism, 85, 135, 144, 150, 156
	of infants, 25–26
Basketball star (story), 58–59
Basley, Hannah, 113
Bath (story), 156–57
Behavior, control of, 27
	cycle of, 28
	and doctrine, 155
	study of, 26, 152
Beliefs, 24
Benson, Ezra Taft, 15, 16
Benthin, Johan H., 18
Bethesda, 30, 31, 34
Bible, 5, 55, 92, 93, 102, 118,
	131
Bishops, 58, 96, 103, 104, 144,
	145, 163
Blessings, 54, 65
Boggs, Lilburn W., 172
Book of Mormon, 5, 63, 74, 92,
	93, 118, 120, 131
Box Elder Stake, 113
Boys, teaching of, 11
Branch presidents, 144, 145
Breen, John, 160–61, 162, 163
Brigham City, Utah, 68
Brigham Young University, 72

— C —

Callis, Charles A., 48–49
Canada, 53
Cannon, George Q., 183
	on temples lessening Satan's
		power, 150–51
Career training, 63–70

Carthage Jail (Ill.), 156
Celestial kingdom, 150
Celestial marriage. *See* Marriage
Cerebral palsy (story), 32
Charity, 99–100
Chastity, 20
Children, baptism of, 25–26
	with disabilities, 30–36
	false doctrines about, 24–26
	and Jesus Christ, 22–24
	marriage provides shelter for, 26
	reverence for, 26
	sacrificing for, 7
	teaching of, 4–5, 20, 129
	wayward, 6, 10, 85, 125–26,
		155
Choice. *See* Agency
Christus statue, 18
Church schools, 71–77, 132
Clark, J. Reuben, on Apostles,
	46–47
	on divine authority, 43
Clean, being washed, 152–59
Coach driver (story), 136
Coffee, 135
Colonies, 77
"Come, All Ye Sons of God"
	(hymn), 55
Comforter. *See* Holy Ghost
Communication disorders, 30
Compassion, 20
Compulsion, 28
Concordance, Bible, 131
Conferences, 39–44
Confession, 54, 163
Confirmation, 85, 144
Congress, 174
Consequences, 135
Consistency, 11
Contraception, 6
Control, 27, 128–33
Copenhagen, Denmark, 18
Corinne, Utah, 113

Council meetings, 42
Courage, 20, 30, 56, 66, 130
Courtesy, 67
Covenants, 3, 8, 13, 54, 125–26, 140, 169, 178
Cowdery, Oliver, 107
Critics, 54–55
    of Church leaders, 49–50
Crocodiles, spiritual, 134
Cross-references, 5
Crucifixion, 139
Cults, 77
Curriculum, overhauling of, 5

— D —

Dam collapse (story), 80–82
Danish woman (story), 9
Dead, work for the, 143, 176, 177
Death, 24, 139
Deceivers, 77–78, 102–4
Dedication, 75–76
Denmark, 18, 83
Dependability, 67
Depwade Union Workhouse, 115
Determination, 130
Devil. *See* Satan
Disabilities, 30–36
    and missionary work, 59
Disappointment, 90
Discernment, 48–49, 96
Disease, 24
Divorce, 6, 24
Doctrine, 7, 24–28, 31, 152, 155
Doctrine and Covenants, 5, 92, 94, 118
Donner Party, 160–61
Dreams, 90

— E —

Editor at conference (story), 40–41

Edmunds-Tucker Act, 174
Edom, 43
Education, 63–70, 71–77
    and pride, 74–75
Egypt, 138–39
Elders, 96, 100, 103, 104, 147
Electricity, 174
Eli, 10
Elijah, 176
Elisha, 64
Embarrassment, 32
Employment training, 63–70
Endowment (ordinance), 143, 145–46, 147, 150, 179
Endurance, 30
England, 175
Environment, moral, 120–27
Ephesians, 89
Eternal marriage. *See* Marriage
Evans, Edwin, 175
Evil spirits, 89–90, 102–3, 108
Evolution, 122–23
Exaltation, 110, 163
Example, 83
    bad, 6, 10–11
Exceptions, 6
Expectations, 11
Experience, 116, 179
Extermination order, 172
Ezekiel, on fathers, 10

— F —

Faculty, 75–76
Faddism, 137
Failure, 9, 63, 90
Fairbanks, John, 175
Faith, and gifts of the Spirit, 103, 104–6
    going forward with, 139–40
    and learning, 63
    as preparation for ordinances, 144

and revelation, 87–88
and the Salt Lake Temple, 174
shield of, 19–20
and signs, 101–2, 110
and study, 71
False doctrine, 24–26
False revelation, 77–78
False spirits, 89–90
Fame, 115–17
Families, and following Church
    leaders, 51
God's plan for happy, 20–21
leadership in, 7
and marriage, 140
ministry of prophets and apostles
    leads to, 19
reverence for relationships in, 10
Satan's purpose is to destroy, 3
single-parent, 6
successful, 124–26
teaching children in, 129–30
and wayward husbands and fa-
    thers, 4, 6–8, 10–11
Family history, 97, 114–15, 151,
    175
Family home evening, 4
Fanaticism, 137
Farmington Bay, Utah, 174
Far West, Mo., 168, 169
Fasting, 166
Fatherhood, responsibilities of,
    10–14
Father in Heaven. *See* Heavenly
    Father
Fathers, and consistency, 11
expectations of, 11
hammer shields of faith, 19
and honoring the priesthood, 11
responsibility of, 7
wayward, 4, 5–8, 10–11
Favoritism, 73
Fear, 90
Feelings, 87, 107

Fidelity, 7
First Presidency, and conferences,
    41–42
on institute, 73
issued epistle about temples,
    179–83
ordered settlements evacuated,
    172–73
sustaining of the, 15
united with the Twelve, 50–51
was in place by 1833, 46
on the welfare program, 65
Footnotes, 131
Forgiveness, 20, 28, 126, 154,
    161–67
Fortune. *See* Wealth
France, 175
Franklin, Benjamin, on experience,
    116
Free agency. *See* Agency
Freedom, misuse of word, 4
Freedom of choice. *See* Agency

— G —

Gambling, 122
Gathering, the, 71–73, 77–78
Gender, loosening of laws on, 4
  plain talk about, 6
Genealogy, 97, 114–16, 151, 175
General, four-star (story), 128–29
General Authorities, authority of,
    43–44
and conferences, 40–41
heed counsel of, 51
parents seek help from, 10
prominence of, 117
receive many suggestions for
    good causes, 66
sustaining of, 49–50
See also Apostles; First Presi-
    dency; Presiding Bishopric;
    Prophets; Seventies

General conference, 39–44
 socials after, 113
Germany, 79
Geshem, 55
Gift of the Holy Ghost. *See* Holy
 Ghost
Gifts of the Spirit, 92–110
 and bishops and elders, 96,
 103, 104
 cannot be forced, 98
 carry great responsibility, 108
 deterrents to, 107
 diversity among the, 96–98
 do not come automatically,
 106–7
 and faith, 103, 104–6
 and Gift of the Holy Ghost,
 108–9
 and intellect, 107–8
 testimony of, 109–10
 types of, 92–95
God. *See* Heavenly Father
Gomorrah, 127
Gospel Doctrine (book), 166
Grant, Heber J., on conferences,
 40
Griffith Park, Calif., 154
Guilt, 31, 165

— H —

Hafen, John, 175
Haley, Mary. *See* Sayers, Mary Haley
Handicaps. *See* Disabilities
Happiness, 116, 119, 124, 140,
 154–55, 165
Harman, Edith, 115
Harman, Eleanor Sayers, 115
Hawaii, 130, 156
Healings, 33, 34, 64, 164
Health, 136–37, 139
Heavenly Father, appeared to
 Joseph Smith, 46

God as our, 12, 27, 28, 34, 84,
 123–24
Hinckley, Gordon B., 15, 16, 50
Holy Ghost, 13, 50, 79–83, 138,
 140
 angels speak by power of, 48,
 85, 109
 as the Comforter, 90–91, 138
 gift of the, 85, 108–9, 138
 is a still small voice, 86–87
 See also Gifts of the Spirit
Holy Spirit of Promise, 178
Hope, 164, 166
"Hosanna Anthem," 177
Humiliation, 154
Hunsaker, Faun, 22
Hunter, Howard W., 15, 16
Husbands, responsibilities of, 7, 10
 wayward, 4, 5–8, 10–11

— I —

Idaho, 80–82
Incest, 121
Independence, Mo., 168
Indifference, 107
Indulgence, 129
Infidelity, 121
Institute, 72–73, 131–32
Integrity, 67
Intellect, 107–8, 110
Intelligence, 129
Interviews, 144–45
Iowa, 168
Isaiah, "sins be as scarlet," 162
Israelites, 43, 64, 138

— J —

Jacob (Nephi's brother), on the
 learned, 74–75
 on wayward fathers and husbands, 4, 5–6, 10–11

James, 46
James (Apostle), 42
Jerusalem, 30, 55
Jesus Christ, appeared in Kirtland
    Temple, 176
    appeared to Joseph Smith, 46
    atonement of, 28, 152, 155–57,
        164, 165, 166–67
    and children, 22–24
    chose twelve Apostles, 45
    on the Comforter, 91
    on critics, 49
    on disabilities, 31
    on heeding the Apostles, 51
    on the Holy Ghost, 138
    "I have chosen you," 50
    as the Lamb of God, 139
    Lorenzo Snow's vision of, 175
    "many mansions," 150
    on repentance, 155
    on signs, 101
    spirit of, 84–85
    on truth, 128–29
    witnesses of, 48, 51–52
John (Apostle), 42, 46
    on the fiery serpent, 44
    on sin, 154
Johnson's Ranch, Calif., 160, 162
Johnston's army, 172
Jokes, 155
Jonas, 102
Jordan River, 64
Joshua, 17
Jubilee box (story), 113–14
Judas Iscariot, 18

— K —

Kane, Thomas L., 168, 172
Kava. *See* Native Drinks
Keys, priesthood, 16, 18, 45, 46,
    148–50, 169
Kimball, Spencer W., 18, 132

on cleaning up, 65
on education, 76
on personal revelation, 87
Kingdom of God, 118
King (story), 136
Kirtland Temple, 168, 176, 177
Knowledge, 139

— L —

Laman, 107
Lamanites, 98
Land mines, 134
Langley Field, Va., 152–53
Language, 154–55
Language of the Spirit, 79–83
Last days, 84
Laws, moral, 123, 124
    physical, 123
Leaders, Church, 77–78
    See also General Authorities
Leadership, of the family, 7
Learning, 63–70, 71–77, 84
    disabilities, 30, 73
    and pride, 74–75
Lee, Harold B., 48, 166
    on the gathering, 72
    on the home, 125
Lemuel, 107
Leprosy, 64
Line of authority, 16, 21
Liquor, 135
Logan Temple, 150
London, England, 114
Loneliness, 32
Los Angeles, Calif., 153–54
Love, 166
    Christian, 164–65

— M —

Malachi, on Elijah, 176
Marriage, covenants, 140

eternal, 3, 125–26, 146–48
fidelity in, 7
laws on, 26
loosening of laws on, 4
Materialism, 117
Matthew (Apostle), 42
McConkie, Bruce R., on the gath-
ering, 72
McKay, David O., on conferences,
39
on the home, 125
Medical school (story), 56–57
Medication, 137
Meetings, reduction of, 7
and the Spirit, 100
Melchizedek Priesthood, 46, 54,
147, 172
Mendoza, Argentina, 32
Mexico City, 72
Military (story), 129, 137, 152–54
Miracles, 31, 82
Missionaries, 53, 55, 83, 108,
133, 175
Missionary work, financial prepa-
ration for, 58
priesthood duty of, 55–60
sacrifices for, 56–57
worthiness for, 57–59
Missouri, 172
Moderation, 136–37
Modesty, 121, 146
Monkey (story), 27
Moral agency. *See* Agency
Moral conduct, 27
Moral environment, 120–27
Morality, 120–21, 122, 123, 124,
127
Moral values, 3–4, 67, 120, 121,
122, 132, 152
Mormon, on angels, 48
on baptism of infants, 25–26
on gifts of the Spirit, 104–5,
105–6

Moroni, and baptism of infants, 25
on Elijah, 176
on evil spirits, 102
on gifts of the Spirit, 94
on meetings and the Spirit, 100
on spiritual gifts, 99
on spiritual promptings, 90
Mortality, 34
Moses, 17, 43–44, 54, 138
Mothers, polish and fit shield of
faith, 19
Music, 88–89

— N —

Naaman, 64–65
Name, honoring of one's, 12–13
Native drinks, 136
Natural law, 31
Nauvoo Temple, 51, 168–69, 169,
176–77
Neglect, 6, 28
parental, 6
Nehemiah, 55
Nephi, on angels, 48
"feel his words," 107–8
on feeling the Spirit, 87
on the Holy Ghost, 109, 140
on "simpleness of the way," 44
was led by the Spirit, 91
Nikko Kanko, Japan, 129
North Dakota, 132

— O —

Obedience, 41, 104, 110, 127,
128, 129, 136, 137, 138, 139
Obscurity, 117
Occupational training, 63–70
Omaha, Nebr., 132
Ono, plains of, 55
Opposition, 54, 56, 117, 150–51,
174

Ordinances, 53, 54–55, 56,
    143–44, 150, 176, 178
Ordinary, the, 65, 67, 70

— P —

Packer, Donna Smith, 73, 114
Packer, Sarah Adeline Wight, 113
Parents, help children be worthy,
    56–58
  help for, 129–30
  love of, 165
  measure of successful, 124–26
  must set children free, 133
  seek help from General Authori-
    ties, 10
  should support teachers, 132
  should teach their children,
    4–5, 20
  and teaching the gospel, 130–31
Passover, 139
Patience, 11
Paul (Apostle), "all men most mis-
    erable," 34
  on the Apostasy, 45
  on apostles and prophets, 45
  "body is the temple," 138
  on last days, 20
  on songs, 89
  on spiritual gifts, 99
  statue of, 18
Pearl of Great Price, 5
Perdition, 162, 164
Personal revelation. *See* Revelation
Peter (Apostle), on filthy conversa-
    tion, 154
  received keys, 18, 45, 148–49
  restored priesthood with James
    and John, 46
  was a fisherman, 42
Pharaoh, 138
Philosophy, 27–28
Physical disabilities. *See* Disabilities

Physical laws, 123
Pinegar, Rex D., 18
Plan of salvation, 5, 7, 8, 154
Poems, 157–59
Politics, 122
  and General Authorities, 42
Poorhouse (story), 114
Poor Richard, on experience, 116
Pornography, 121
Posterity, message to, 113–14
Poverty, 117
Power, 9, 53–54
Practice, 130–31
Pratt, Lorus, 175
Pratt, Orson, 171
Pratt, Parley P., "The Morning
    Breaks," 171
Prayer, 85, 110, 140, 155, 166
  in public schools, 3
Premortal life, 34
Preparation, 84
President of the Church, and reve-
    lation, 47
  holds all keys, 149
  is able to have all gifts, 104
Presiding Bishopric, 46, 52
Pride, 74–75
Priesthood, 12, 53–60
  authority, 77, 169
  honoring the, 11, 54
  keys, 16, 18, 45, 46, 148–50,
    169
  line of authority, 16–17, 20
  missionary duty of the, 56–60
Principles, of conduct, 7
"Pro-choice" argument, 122
Procreation, 120–21
Promises, 135–36, 137, 138
Promptings, 87
  See also Holy Ghost
Prophets, receive revelation, 5
  and the Salt Lake Temple, 169
  stand at head of Church, 9

sustaining of, 17
as watchmen, 4
Public schools, 72
prayers in, 3
Pullham, Norfolk, England, 115
Punishment, 163

— Q —

Quorum of the Twelve Apostles.
See Apostles

— R —

Railroads, 171
Recommends, temple, 144–45
Redemption, 138–39, 177
Rejection, 32
Relief Society, 113
Relief Society president (story), 6
Remembrance, 127
Repentance, 20, 25, 28, 54, 126,
144, 147, 154, 155–57,
162–64
Reporter at conference, 40–41
Respect, 67
Responsibility, 135
Restitution, 163–64
Restoration, of the body, 33–36
of the gospel, 46, 179
Resurrection, 33, 34, 36
Retardation. *See* Disabilities
Returned missionaries, 108
Revelation, Church ordered by,
9–10
and faith, 87–88
false, 77–78, 89–90, 102–4
and music, 88–89
order of, 90
personal, 84, 86–90, 138
and prayer, 85
and the President of the Church,
47

prophets and apostles receive, 5
and reverence, 89
and the still small voice,
86–87
and the Word of Wisdom, 88,
138
Reverence, for children, 26
for family relationships, 10
and music, 89
for the priesthood, 53
shield of faith made from, 20
Rexburg, Idaho, 82
Richards, LeGrand, 175
Riches. *See* Wealth
Ricks College, 72
Ridicule, 31–32, 54–55
Righteousness, 115–16
Rocky Mountains, 171
Romney, Marion G., on personal
revelation, 87
Rules, 6

— S —

Sacrament, 139, 147
Sacramento Valley, Calif., 160
Sacrifice, 7, 175
Salt Lake City, Utah, 178
Salt Lake Temple, 169–75, 177,
179
Salt Lake Valley, Utah, 169
Sanballat, 55
Satan, attacks moral values, 121
breaking free from, 126
and compulsion, 28
desires to destroy families, 3–4
desires to destroy unity of the
faith, 19
and false revelation, 89–90
fights against temples, 150–51,
172, 173
Satanic rituals, 124
Sayers, Edward, 115

Sayers, Eleanor. *See* Harman, Eleanor Sayers
Sayers, Mary Haley, 114–15
Schools, 71–77, 132
  sex education in, 121
Scriptures, are the constant, 7
  curriculum centered on, 5, 131
  new editions of, 5
  translations of, 5
Sealings, 125–26, 143, 146–50
Self-control, 128, 129
Selfishness, 35
Self-reliance, 66, 77
Self-sufficiency, 11–12
Seminaries, 72, 131–33
Seminary graduation (story), 32, 130
Serpent, fiery, 43–44
Seventies, 18, 46, 52
Shakers, 140n
Shakespeare, William, on asking your heart, 89
Shame, 153–54
Shield of faith, 19–20
Sierra Nevada Mountains, 160
Signs, seeking after, 101–2, 110
  of the times, 77
Sin, 124, 126–27, 154–56, 163
Singles, 6
Smith, George Albert, dream of, 12–13
Smith, Hyrum, 156
Smith, John, 40
Smith, Joseph, on authority, 90
  on "decision of character," 35
  on false spirits, 89–90
  Joseph F. Smith's dream of, 157
  on the mind's enlargement, 35
  Moroni appeared to, 176
  on ordinances, 150
  on pardoning mercy, 166
  on personal revelation, 86–87
  on priesthood keys, 16

  on redemption, 177
  and the Restoration, 46
  on wayward children, 125
Smith, Joseph F., 183
  dreams of washing himself clean, 156–57
  on "saviors on Mount Zion," 166
Smith, Joseph Fielding, on disabilities, 33
  on witnesses of Jesus Christ, 48
Snow, Lorenzo, had vision of Christ, 175
Social agencies, 10
Sodom, 127
Songs, 88–89
Sorrow, 90
Southern States Mission, 22
Spirit of Christ, 84–85
"Spirit of God, The" (hymn), 177
Stake missions, 59
Stake presidents, 104
Study, 86
Success, 119, 124–26
Sugar City, Idaho, 81
Sustaining, 15, 17, 49–50, 78
Symbolism, of the Salt Lake Temple, 171–72
  of temples, 146
Sympathy, 165

— T —

Taylor, John, on conferences, 42
Tea, 135
Teachers, 13–14, 56–58, 75–76, 132, 133
Teaching, 4–5, 7
Temple marriage. *See* Marriage
Temple recommends, 144–45
Temples, 168–84
  opposition to, 150–51
  ordinances and covenants of, 54

response to critics of, 54–55
sacred ordinance of, 143–44
as a school, 145–46
sealings in, 125–26, 146–50
and the Word of Wisdom, 135, 145
worthiness for, 144–45
See also individual temples
Temple Square, 171, 172–73
Temporal support, 7, 11
Temptation, 56, 89–90
Terence, on fathers as judges, 11
Terry, Jane, gives advice to teachers, 13–14
Testimony, 59, 91, 109–10, 157–59
Teton Dam, Idaho, 80–82
Thorvaldsen, Bertel, 18
Tithing, 41, 76, 145
Tobacco, 135
Tobiah, 55
Tooele, Utah, 175
Topical Guide, 5, 131
Tradition, 73–74
Trials. *See* Opposition
Truth, 128–29
Tuttle, A. Theodore, 58
Two Dogs, Sister, 132

— U —

United Society of Believers in Christ's Second Appearing, 140n
Unity, 50–51
Utah, 174
Utah War, 172

— V —

Values, 3–4, 67, 120, 121, 122, 132, 152
Virtues, ordinary, 67

Visions, 90
Vocational training, 63–70

— W —

Warning voice, 79–82
"Washed Clean" (poem), 157–59
Washington, D.C., 166
Wayward children. *See* Children
Wealth, 115–19
Weeks, William, 169
Welfare program, 65
Whitney, Orson F., on wayward children, 125
Widtsoe, John A., on temples, 145–46
Willard Ward, Idaho, 80
Winter Quarters, Nebr., 160, 169
Wisdom, 11, 64
Witnesses, 47–48, 51–52
Wives, as partners, 7
Woodruff, Wilford, epistle of, 183
and the Salt Lake Temple, 171, 175
on the Salt Lake Temple, 170
Woods, James F., 175
Word of Wisdom, 88, 134–40
Work ethic, 69–70
Workhouse school (story), 114
Worldliness, 107
World War II, 152–54
Worthiness, 57–59, 144–45

— Y —

"Ye Elders of Israel" (hymn), 56
Young, Brigham, "bells of hell," 172
on experience, 179
led the pioneers, 160
on righteous parents, 126
and the Salt Lake Temple, 171, 172

on the Salt Lake Temple, 169,
170, 173
on spiritual gifts, 98–99
Young, John, on conferences, 40
Youth, 134

— Z —

Zion, 71, 119